CURIOUS EVENTS
IN HISTORY

Library of Congress Cataloging-in-Publication Data Available

1 2 3 4 5 6 7 8 9 10

Published in 2008 by Sterling Publishing Co., Inc.

387 Park Avenue South, New York, NY 10016

Copyright © 2007 JW Cappelens Forlag under license from Gusto
Company AS
Written by Michael Powell
Executive editor: James Tavendale
Original concept by James Tavendale
Designed by Allen Boe
Illustrations AnnDréa Boe, Scanpix,© Wikipedia Commons
Indexer: Carla Johnson
Printed in China

Distributed in Canada by Sterling Publishing
c/o Canadian Manda Group, 165 Dufferin Street
Toronto, Ontario, Canada M6K 3h6

For information about custom editions, special sales, premium
and corporate purchases, please contact Sterling Special Sales
Department at 800-805-5489 or specialsales@sterlingpub.com

Manufactured in China

Sterling ISBN: 978-1-4027-6307-6

CURIOUS EVENTS IN HISTORY

Michael Powell

STERLING
New York / London
www.sterlingpublishing.com

CONTENTS

The Hat That Caused a Riot

INTRODUCTION

History isn't as boring as the textbooks would lead you to believe. Scattered between the famous historical milestones are tiny gems waiting to be discovered. These fascinating carbuncles contain all the bits of history they didn't tell you about in school.

Here are forty of the most curious events in history, from a thirty-eight minute war, to the time when a top hat caused a riot! Forgotten, bizarre, weird, and obscure facts, firsts and lasts, some peculiar inventions, and a few unpalatable truths all make up the fabric of the secret history that we unfold here.

If you thought you knew all you needed to know about history you will be amazed at the gaps in your knowledge as you discover, among other things, which U.S. president was killed by his own doctors, who was the last person executed in the Tower of London, and how murder came to America aboard the *Mayflower*.

Somebody once said, "If you do not like the past, change it." You'll be surprised how often history has been rewritten in favor of the remembered, while cutting the long forgotten and casually overlooked out of the story altogether.

THE BATTLE OF KADESH AND THE PHARAOH'S BIG WHITE LIE

Pharaohs ruled Egypt for over 3,000 years, but one of them stands out. For sixty-seven years Ramesses II reigned over the largest empire in the world, outliving many of his children. His crowning achievement, however, was his self-created legend. He was an ancient master of "spin," best shown by how he rewrote history to make himself appear a great hero after his poor performance at the Battle of Kadesh.

Background of the Battle

For several centuries prior to the reign of Ramesses II, the Egyptian, Mittani, and Hittite empires had been in conflict, with Egypt continually ceding land. During the reign of Ramesses's father, Seti I, the Canaanite city of Kadesh was under Egyptian control, but it had been lost again by the time he came to power.

RAMESSES II

The Battle of Kadesh

The Battle of Kadesh took place in 1274 B.C. between the army of Ramesses II and the Hittite forces of Muwatalli II at the Orontes River in present-day Syria. It was the biggest chariot battle ever fought, and it ended in a stalemate. If anything, the Hittites had the upper hand, but Ramesses's version of his "victory" is the most epic example of spin-doctoring in the ancient world.

The Hittite king Muwatalli hid his troops behind the hill at Kadesh. Ramesses believed that they were many miles away to the north. As soon as he discovered that his catastrophic misjudgment had led him into a trap, Ramesses instructed two of his divisions to cross the Orontes to help him. Before they could arrive, 2,500 of Muwatalli's chariots attacked them and then turned on Ramesses's division. The pharaoh narrowly escaped capture, and it was only after the arrival of an army from Amurru, which drove the Hittites back, that a truce was called.

Ramesses had suffered many casualties and couldn't capture any more territory. It would be another five years before his army was strong enough to attack the Hittites again, and his defeat caused several revolts within the Egyptian empire. So he set his spin machine into action to rewrite history on an extraordinary scale.

Ancient Spin

In his book, *Chronicle of the Pharaohs*, Peter Clayton sums up Ramesses's ruling ethos: "During his long reign of sixty-seven years, everything was done on a grand scale. No other pharaoh constructed so many temples or erected so many colossal statues and obelisks. No other pharaoh sired so many children. Ramesses's 'victory' over the Hittites at Kadesh was celebrated in one of the most repeated Egyptian texts ever put on record."

To rewrite history, Ramesses commissioned legions of artisans to carve epic depictions of the Battle of Kadesh in temples around the empire. They depicted him as a god-like warrior, singlehandedly charging the enemy and driving them back, after being abandoned by his troops. In total, he commissioned no fewer than ten inscriptions, a longer "poem," and a shorter "bulletin" with additional reliefs. Many of them can still be seen today, such as those in the magnificent Abu Simbel Temple in Nubia, or at the Temple of Luxor, where the Pharaoh's big white lie, set in stone, still stands the test of time.

THE UNFORTUNATE DEATH OF DRACO

Draco was the first law scribe of Athens in the seventh century B.C. The word "draconian," which is often attributed to measures or punishments that are unusually severe or cruel, is named for Draco, because the laws he imposed were so harsh. Despite this, he was very popular; in fact, his popularity was the direct cause of his curious and untimely death.

The School of Athens

The Athenian Eupatrids

The eupatrids were the Athenian noblemen. They made all the legal decisions and were the enforcers of laws which, until Draco wrote them down, were arbitrary and inconsistent. By 621 B.C. the Athenian people were no longer willing to accept these unwritten laws, so Draco was instructed to codify Athenian law for the first time. He didn't create the laws; he merely standardized them and wrote them down.

Draconian Laws

The laws were particularly ruthless and recording them highlighted their harshness. Anyone who was in debt to a social superior could be forced into slavery. Owing to one's inferiors also merited punishment, albeit a lesser one. The death penalty often was applied for minor offenses. When Draco was asked for his opinion, he stated that the death penalty was appropriate for stealing something as insignificant as a cabbage. Plutarch describes Draco's attitude towards the death penalty in his "Life of Solon": "And Draco himself, they say, being asked why he made death the penalty for most offenses, replied that in his opinion the lesser ones deserved it, and for the greater ones no heavier penalty could be found."

Draco's Death

Draco's death is one of the most curious events in ancient history. In 590 B.C. a testimonial was held in honor of the great law scribe at the theater of Athena. As Draco made his grand entrance at the open-air arena, thousands of over-enthusiastic supporters threw their hats and cloaks on him, as the customary sign of appreciation and respect. Because there were so many attendees, the pile of clothing was overwhelming. By the time he was rescued from beneath the enormous pile of discarded garments, Draco had suffocated to death. If he hadn't been so popular he might have escaped with his life.

CALIGULA MOURNS THE DEATH OF HIS SISTER

Roman Emperor Caligula was so distraught after the death of his sister Drusilla that he imposed a year of mourning. Throughout the Roman Empire, citizens were forbidden to conduct business, dine with their family, cut their hair, or take a bath. The penalty for contravention was death.

Who Was Caligula?

Born Gaius Julius Caesar Augustus Germanicus on August 31, 12, Caligula was the third Roman Emperor, ruling from A.D. 37 to 41. He is best remembered as an eccentric, depraved, and cruel despot. His early reign was quite promising and he was a popular ruler, despite his later downward spiral. After coming to power, he declared an end to treason, revived free elections, recalled exiles, and put on lavish public entertainments.

Thrasyllus, the soothsayer of his predecessor Tiberius, had predicted that Caligula had "no more chance of becoming Emperor than of riding a horse across the Gulf of Baiae," so to prove him spectacularly wrong, Caligula stretched a two-mile pontoon bridge from Baiae to the neighboring port of Puteoli and rode over the water, wearing the breastplate of Alexander the Great.

Imperial Insanity

The Roman historian Suetonius branded Caligula a "monster" and detailed many instances of his lunacy. He is alleged to have had an incestuous relationship with all three of his sisters, but his youngest sister Drusilla was his favorite. He is also alleged to have appointed his horse, Incitatus, to a seat on the senate and attempted to appoint it to the position of consul. At gladiatorial games, if there weren't enough convicts to fight the lions, he would have a handful of spectators thrown into the arena. At night he wandered around his palace commanding the sun to rise. He opened a brothel in his palace and slept with the wives of Senate members after inviting them to dine. They could do nothing when he bragged of his conquests, unless they wanted to lose their lives. He was anxious about hair loss and made it a crime for anyone to look down on him from above. He also demanded that rich men leave all their possessions to him in their wills, then had them murdered. He was finally assassinated by his own guards in A.D. 41.

How Did Drusilla Die?

There are several explanations for her death on June 10, A.D. 38. The most mundane is that she died of a fever which was rampant in Rome at the time; another is that she died from loss of blood; the most famous account is given by Suetonius, who claimed that Drusilla became pregnant with Caligula's child and that he disemboweled her, believing the unborn baby to be divine and therefore a threat to his throne.

Goddess Cult

Caligula never recovered from Drusilla's death and declared her a goddess, a representation of Aphrodite, the goddess of love, beauty, and sexual rapture. She was given a lavish public funeral which Caligula was too distraught to attend. He left Rome and retreated to his villa at Alba, where he refused to wash or cut his beard and hair. He declared a period of public mourning (*iustitium*) with fatal consequences to any who failed to observe it. During this time all business activity and public entertainments were suspended. A man was executed for selling hot water since, until Drusilla was buried, drinking was forbidden (hot water was used for mixing with wine).

Caligula commissioned a golden statue of Drusilla for the Senate house that was the same size as the statue of Venus in her temple. She was given her own shrine with twenty priests of both sexes. In the future, her birthday was observed by a two-day festival where 500 bears and elephants were killed, games were held, and her statue was paraded through Rome.

Palace of Tiberius Caesar and Caligula

THE ORIGIN OF VALENTINE'S DAY

Every year on February 14, millions of people around the world celebrate Valentine's Day by sending love tokens to the objects of their affection. The origin and history of this lovers' day is curious: it dates back to a pagan festival in ancient Rome, and there are at least three Saint Valentines.

Who Was Saint Valentine?

All three Saint Valentines were martyred, and all three are listed in early martyrologies (accounts of martyrs) under the date of February 14. Little is known about any of them. One died in Africa. Another, who served as bishop of Interamna (modern Terni) in the late second century A.D., was killed during the persecution of Emperor Aurelian; he is buried on the Via Flaminia and his relics are at the Basilica of Saint Valentine in Terni. The third Saint Valentine was a Christian priest in Rome, who was martyred in A.D. 269 for defying the wishes of Emperor Claudius II. The emperor was having trouble recruiting new soldiers for his many military campaigns. He attributed this to men wanting to stay at home with their lovers, so he canceled all marriages and engagements in Rome. Saint Valentine was arrested when he continued to marry couples in secret. He was condemned to be beaten to death with clubs and decapitated. He, too, is buried on the Via Flaminia. His relics are at the Church of Saint Praxed in Rome.

The Lupercalia

At the time of Saint Valentine's death, Christianity had yet to completely supplant pagan worship in Rome. In the third century A.D., packs of wild wolves roaming outside the city were a menace to local shepherds and their flocks. The Roman god Lupercus was believed to oversee the flocks and keep them safe, so every February 15, for several centuries, the Romans had observed a feast in honor of Lupercus, called the Lupercalia. During the celebrations the names of young women were put into a box and drawn at random by young men. The couples then paired off for the year.

De-paganization of Valentine's Day

In A.D. 496, as part of the Catholic Church's efforts to Christianize pagan practices, Pope Gelasius changed the date of Lupercalia to February 14, and renamed it in honor of St. Valentine. The practice of drawing names from the box was modified: saints' names were

used instead of women's, and the young men who drew them were expected to spend the year emulating the life of their chosen saint. By the fourteenth century lovers' names were again being used, although the church briefly attempted (without success) to reintroduce saintly names in the sixteenth century. Although Valentine's Day is hugely popular today, the confusion over its origins led the Catholic Church, in 1969, to drop St. Valentine's Day from the Roman calendar of official, worldwide Catholic feasts.

Valentine's Day is interesting historically because, as with many Christian festivals, it began as a pagan feast but was appropriated by the Church and de-paganized. The Church subsequently abandoned it, and the day is once again a secular celebration. Most people today are unaware of Valentine's Day's pagan and religious past stretching back over two thousand years.

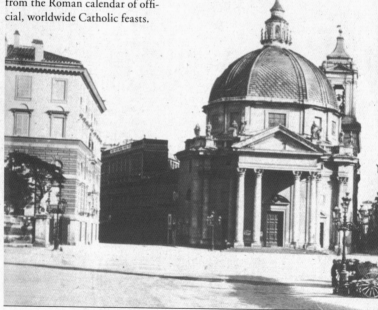

The entrance to Rome from the Via Flaminia

POWDERED EGYPTIAN MUMMIES

Human remains have been used as medicine for thousands of years. The Ebers papyrus, which is 3,500 years old, describes how to use the brain of a dead man to treat diseases of the eye. The medicinal use of Egyptian mummies was first recorded in the tenth century A.D. and trade in therapeutic mummy dust was a thriving business from the twelfth to the nineteenth centuries.

How Many Mummies Did the Egyptians Make?

It has been estimated that the Egyptians made half a million mummies prior to the Greco-Roman era. When the classical Greeks discovered the ruins of Egyptian civilization, mummies were all that remained of their funerary know-how, which intrigued and mystified subsequent civilizations.

Whose Bright Idea Was It?

The tenth-century Persian physician, Avicenna, recommended the use of ground mummy as a cure for rashes, coughs, constipation, paralysis, diseases of the spleen and liver, and a host of other ailments. As one critic wryly observed, his "list might have been shorter if he had told us when this panacea was not effective."

Mummies were ground into powder and made into a tincture, elixir, treacle, or balsam, and even taken straight. It is not known when exactly mummies were first used medicinally on a commercial scale, but it likely began with Jewish traders in twelfth-century Alexandria.

Mummies were collected and shipped across the Mediterranean and became the staple cure-all of apothecaries. Mummies were especially popular in France. Catherine of Medici's chaplain raided tombs at Saqqara. Francis I of France didn't leave the house without a packet of mummy dust; every day, he took a pinch of mummy with rhubarb, in the belief that it would make him invulnerable to assassins. However, the practice was not without its detractors, including the leading sixteenth-century French surgeon Ambroise Paré, who argued, "this wicked kind of Drugge doth nothing help the diseased . . . but it also inferres [causes] many troublesome symptoms, as the paine of the heart or stomacke, vomiting and stinke of the mouth."

Fake Mummies

So great was the demand for mummies that by the fifteenth century tens of thousands of genuine mummies had been used and supply was running short. There were probably more fakes around than the genuine article. A physician to the King of Navarre, Guy de la Fontaine, visited the shop of the chief merchant of mummies in Alexandria, where he discovered that the entire stock of forty specimens had been prepared in the last four years from the corpses of slaves, criminals, and deceased hospital patients. The corpses had been filled with bitumen and left in the sun to harden. Seventeenth-century sources advised buyers how to spot a true mummy from a fake. The best mummy powder was fine, shiny, and black, not full of bones and dirt, and it did not stink of bitumen when it was burned.

The Last Mummy

As late as 1908 medicinal mummy could still be ordered from the catalog of the pharmaceutical company E. Merck, which advertised "Genuine Egyptian mummy, as long as the supply lasts."

Don't settle for anything less than the real thing.

25% OFF **GENUINE EGYPTIAN MUMMY** AS LONG AS THE SUPPLY LASTS

THE FIRST KAMIKAZE

In 1944, when Japanese suicide pilots began crashing their planes into American ships during World War II, the word "kamikaze" achieved worldwide notoriety. It translates as "divine wind," and in the Japanese national psyche it is both a powerful symbol of the destruction of enemy invaders, and a testament to a country whose people so sanctify it that they are willing to die for it. However, the origins of the kamikaze date back to the thirteenth century and have nothing to do with air war: the Japanese coined the term when they were saved on two occasions by fateful storms that prevented a Mongol invasion and depleted the Mongol fleet.

The Mongol Invasions

In the late thirteenth century, Kublai Khan, grandson of Genghis Khan, ruled over the largest empire in the world, encompassing Russia, the Middle East, central Asia, and eventually China. He wanted to make Japan a tributary state, so in 1274 he launched the fleets from the Korean peninsula and China to arrive in Japan in the sheltered Hakata Bay, in what is today Fukuoka City in north Kyushu.

KUBLAI KHAN

The samurai warriors of Japan were no match for the superior weaponry and battle tactics of the Mongol armies. When the Mongol detachments came ashore, they were met by samurai archers who were accustomed to firing at long range in individual combat. The Mongols advanced to the sound of drums, bells, and war cries, which frightened the Japanese horses, and the Mongols fired clouds of arrows and used catapults to launch devastating gunpowder bombs. The Japanese were saved only by a storm during the night which severely damaged the Mongol fleet at anchor and forced them to return to Korea.

After the failure of the first invasion, the Japanese spent several years fortifying their coastal defenses, including building a large stone wall along the most vulnerable areas. However, when the Mongols invaded again in 1281, they had a much larger army and a fleet of over 4,000 vessels. The fleet landed on two islands in Hakata bay and spent a week attacking. Once again it looked as though the Japanese were going to be conquered. To the surprise of both armies, on July 30, a typhoon blew up again and destroyed the Mongol fleet, leaving few survivors, since most of the army was still onboard, and thousands more were subsequently killed by the Japanese. The Mongol ships had been chained together to form a flotilla, which in the chaos of the storm made it very difficult for them to escape to deeper water. Only one-third of the 140,000-strong Mongol army escaped the slaughter.

What made the kamikaze even more significant was that when the Mongol invasion fleet was advancing on Japan, its religious leaders had been fervently praying for deliverance. Their prayers had been answered. The Mongols never again mounted serious attack.

THE FARCICAL FUNERAL OF WILLIAM THE CONQUEROR

William the Conqueror is famous for defeating King Harold at the Battle of Hastings in 1066. The details surrounding William's death and funeral are less universally known. After a freak accident while riding his horse, he suffered a slow and painful death, and his funeral was the most undignified and disastrous royal send-off in European history.

Early Life

Born in 1027, William was the illegitimate son of Robert I, Duke of Normandy, and was known by the nickname "William the Bastard." After defeating King Harold, he was crowned King of England on Christmas Day 1066 in Westminster Abbey. He was a respected king, and ruled sternly, but he kept good order in his kingdom. He was also ruthless to his opponents, and introduced beheading as a standard form of execution in 1076.

How Did He Die?

William was very fat. In the summer of 1087, while en route to Rouen in France, he attacked a French garrison at the border town of Mantes. He won the battle, but during the subsequent celebrations his horse reared up, frightened by a glowing ember from the smoldering ruins of the town, and threw the obese king violently against the metal pommel at the front of the saddle, rupturing his intestines.

Slow and Painful Death

After his intestines burst, fecal matter began to seep into William's abdominal cavity and peritonitis took hold. He was carried to Rouen where, for the next five weeks, his body slowly poisoned itself and a putrid abscess filled with pus festered in his abdomen.

He died early on the morning of September 9, 1087, at the age of fifty-nine.

The First Indignity

As soon as he died, his wealthier attendants immediately left, keen to protect their own interests. Those remaining, according to twelfth-century historian Orderic Vitalis, "seized the arms, vessels, clothing, linen, and all the royal furnishings, and hurried away leaving the king's body almost naked on the floor of the house." A knight named Herluin discovered William's corpse and, at his own expense, paid for it to be made ready for a funeral and transported to Caen.

The Second Indignity

As the pallbearers were carrying the coffin to the church, they had to abandon it and run off to fight a fire. They resumed the procession later and brought his body to the church.

The Final Indignity

It was a blisteringly hot summer's day, so the king's obese corpse had rotted more than was customary and had swollen considerably. The assembled bishops transferred his body into a specially-commissioned stone sarcophagus inside the church, only to find that it wouldn't fit. The exasperated attendants tried to squeeze him in by pushing on his stomach, which burst, showering the congregation with pus and rotting intestines. People stampeded for the door, covering their noses and wretching.

NERO'S PAINTED "GROTTO" INSPIRES THE RENAISSANCE

In the fifteenth century, the ground collapsed beneath a young man walking along the Aventine hillside in Rome, and he fell into a strange "grotto" with painted figures on the walls. He had accidentally discovered one of Emperor Nero's most extravagant projects, which had lain buried undisturbed for centuries. The *Domus Aurea* (Golden House) quickly became a must-see for Renaissance artists, who let themselves down on knotted ropes to view the frescoes and even wrote their names on the walls for posterity.

Nero Parties in Style

Nero is famous for his lust for excess. He turned party-throwing into an art form, and after two-thirds of Rome was destroyed by the great fire in A.D. 64, he used the spare land for the site of his extravagant new party-palace. He built a complex of buildings spread over an area of 350 acres. Many of the rooms and hallways were decorated entirely with polished white marble and gold. Stuccoed ceilings and walls were covered with semi-precious stones and veneers of ivory. The palace included vineyards, orchards, gardens, forests with grazing animals, and an artificial lake. Nero also commissioned a colossal 120-foot bronze statue of himself, dressed as the Roman sun god Sol. This Colossus Neronis, as it was called, was displayed outside the main palace entrance.

The principle dining room flanked an octagonal court,

with a huge dome and a giant central oculus to admit light. The ceiling underneath the dome, which could be turned by slaves, rotated like the heavens.

Buried Treasure

After Nero's death in A.D. 68, the Golden House became an embarrassment to his successors; within a decade, it had been stripped of its precious metals and stones, and a large area of the complex was filled in with earth and built over. The Flavian Amphitheatre was built on top of the artificial lake. The destruction of other structures followed, including the Baths of Trajan, and the Temples of Venus in Rome. Within forty years, few traces of the Golden House

remained uncovered; its frescoes lay protected from the corrosive effects of the air for centuries.

Renaissance Attraction

Fourteen hundred years later, the reception for Nero's palace was a different story altogether. The Golden House became a star attraction in Renaissance Rome. Young Roman artists flocked to view the frescoes painted by Fabullus. These freshly redis-covered works inspired painters such as Pinturicchio, Raphael, Michelangelo, and Filippo Lippi. Later famous visitors included Casanova and the Marquis de Sade, all of whom scratched their names on the walls.

Today, the Golden House is closed for restoration and is not expected to be reopened to the public for several years. However, its impact on Renais-sance art can be seen in works such as Raphael's decoration for the loggias in the Vatican. Fabullus's influence extended well into the neoclassical period of the late eighteenth century.

THE PIG-RUMP SPIKE-ORGAN OF LOUIS XI

Fifteenth-century monarch Louis XI was one of the most successful kings of France in terms of uniting the country, and was even nicknamed "Louis the Prudent" for his fiscal circumspection. But he also had a sadistic streak that led to the construction of the most idiosyncratic and cruel musical instrument in history: the pig-rump spike-organ.

A King Noted for His Cruelty

Louis XI owed his success as a monarch to a combination of shrewdness and viciousness. He was the nicknamed *l'universalle araigne* —"the universal spider"—for his ruthless and incessant plotting. Intensely paranoid, he maintained power through a network of spies and he frequently tortured his enemies to death. On one occasion he spared a man from execution on condition that the man serve as a human guinea pig in a gallbladder operation.

Louis loved to hunt. One of his officials, Philippe de Commynes, described his love of the chase: "He was continually at these sports, lodging in the country villages to which his recreations led him, till he was interrupted by business." But Louis's passion for hunting extended to people as well as animals. He organized manhunts in which victims wearing deerskins were chased and then ripped apart by hounds.

Louis was fascinated by animals. When he wasn't hunting them, he kept a large zoo of exotic creatures including an elephant, monkeys, and bears. He kept a tame lioness that often accompanied him on his travels.

An Able Abbot

When he felt melancholy, Louis often amused himself by having pigs dressed up in clothes and wigs and pricked with pins to make them dance and "sing." In 1450 he grew tired of this diversion and commanded the Abbot of Baigne to invent a new and preposterous musical instrument for his amusement: a "concert of swines' voices."

The abbot collected a herd of pigs of differing size and age, from nursing piglets to fully-grown swine. Each animal had its own distinct squeal; thus, when the abbot lined them up in order of pitch, he was able

to construct a rudimentary musical apparatus. The seventeenth-century English writer, Nathaniel Wanley, described the result: "Out of a great number of hogs, of several ages, which he got together, and placed under a tent or pavilion covered with velvet, before which he had a table of wood, painted, with a certain number of hogs, he made an organical instrument, and as he played upon the said keys, with little spikes which pricked the hogs he made them cry in such order and consonance, as highly delighted the king and all his men."

Porco-Forte

In 1839, inventors in Cincinnati, Ohio introduced a musical instrument called the "Porco-Forte." It was designed like a piano, but instead of hammers striking strings, the pressing of a key resulted in the pinching of one of a row of pig's tails. Louis XI's pig-rump spike-organ had anticipated this invention by nearly four hundred years.

EDWARD IV'S MAGIC VISION

History is full of omens and strange portents. To a modern audience, most of them seem like superstitious nonsense, but the extraordinary vision that was witnessed by future King Edward IV and his Yorkist army on a crisp morning in 1461 not only influenced the course of history, but has subsequently been verified by modern scientists.

Where Did It Happen?

In the early hours of Candlemas Day, February 2, 1461 Edward, Earl of March, and his army of about 10,000 men, were camped near the town of Ludlow in a small hamlet called Mortimer's Cross. A month earlier Edward's father, Richard III, and brother Edmund, Earl of Rutland, had been brutally killed by the Lancastrians at the Battle of Wakefield, and their severed heads had been placed on the gates of York. Seeking revenge, eighteen-year-old Edward and his army were about to fight the Lancastrian army in the Battle of Mortimer's Cross. The Lancastrians, led by the Owen Tudor, Earl of Pembroke, and his son, Jasper, had just marched into England from South Wales.

What Did They See?

That crisp and clear morning Edward and his men saw three suns rising in a row. These three suns then quickly joined together as one. The meteorological phenomenon they had witnessed is called a parhelion (also known as a "sundog"). It occurs when sunlight is refracted through microscopic ice crystals, usually when wispy cirrus clouds high in the sky cover the sun, causing two ghost images to appear on either side of it.

Omen of Victory

Edward's troops were distressed, but Edward interpreted the peculiar triple sun as a good omen. According to the *Davies Chronicle*, he rallied them with a speech: "Beeth of good comfort and dreadeth not! This is a good sign, for these three suns betokeneth the Father, the Son and the Holy Ghost, and therefore let us have a good heart, and in the name of Almighty God go we against our enemies!"

Edward also interpreted the vision as indicating that he would soon be reunited with the three surviving York sons—himself, George, and Richard (The Dukes of Clarence and Gloucester, aged twelve and nine, respectively). After Edward's rousing speech, the entire Yorkist army knelt in prayer and then went on to win one of the bloodiest battles of the Wars of the Roses, in which 4,000 Lancastrians were killed.

The battle was a decisive victory; it prevented the Earl of Pembroke from joining up with the main body of Lancastrian forces, proved that Edward was a capable leader, and paved the way for his subsequent coronation. After he was crowned King Edward IV two weeks later, he added the sign of "the sunne in splendour" to his banner as his personal emblem.

Other Omens

At several moments in the past, natural phenomena have altered the course of history. One of the most significant and earliest was a lunar eclipse during the Peloponnesian War, in the fifth century B.C. The Athenians had been blockading the Sicilian city of Syracuse for two years and were about to abandon it, until a lunar eclipse was taken as a bad omen for their departure. They stayed, allowing the Syracusans to break out of the siege and destroy the Athenian fleet and army, which ultimately led to the decline of ancient Greek civilization.

In 1504 a lunar eclipse enabled Christopher Columbus to trick the natives of Jamaica to supply him with food. He was marooned there and was desperately short of supplies, but the locals refused to provide any. Facing starvation, Columbus consulted his shipboard almanac which predicted an imminent eclipse, so he told the natives that God would punish them for their lack of cooperation by blackening the sky. After the eclipse, the natives were over-awed by his power and readily supplied him with food until his rescue several months later.

King Edward IV

THE TRIAL OF THE PIG

In 1494, a pig was put on trial in a French monastery. Its crime was having "entered a house and disfigured a child's face, wherepon the child departed this life." The presiding judge, Jehan Levoisier, declared "that the said porker, now detained as a prisoner and confined in the said abbey, shall be by the master of high works hanged and strangled on a gibbet of wood near and adjoinant to the gallows and place of execution." This wasn't an isolated incident; during the Middle Ages, no animals—from insects to turtledoves—were exempted from paying for the consequences of their actions.

Case Notes

For several centuries animals and insects faced prosecution throughout Europe. They appeared before ecclesiastical and secular courts on charges ranging from criminal damage to murder. They were represented by lawyers, and were afforded the same rights and responsibilities as humans.

The definitive book about this phenomenon, Edward Paysons Evans's *The Criminal Prosecution and Capital Punishment of Animals* (1906), contains dozens of accounts of animal trials. His earliest example is the prosecution of a group of moles in the Valle d'Aosta in A.D. 824, but he even documented a twentieth-century conviction of murder by a dog in Switzerland. Domestic and farm animals frequently fell foul of the law. In 1750, a she-ass was prosecuted for being "taken in the act of coition" with her human owner. She was acquitted for her previous good conduct: she had always "shown herself to be a virtuous and well-behaved" beast. In 1596, the judiciary of Marseilles brought a case against a group of dolphins. In 1542, sixteen cows and a goat were tried in the French town of Rouvre. However, the animal that appears in the dock most frequently in Evans's account is the pig.

Rats Are a Career Maker

Some lawyers established their reputations during important animal trials. In the sixteenth century, French advocate Bartholemew Chassenée defended "some rats, which had been put on trial before the ecclesiastical court of Autun on the charge of having feloniously eaten up and wantonly destroyed the barley crop of that province." He argued that the summons which instructed the rats to appear before the court had not been circulated sufficiently among the rat population, and that the rats could not attend because of "the length and difficulty of the journey and serious perils which attended it," namely, the neighborhood cats. Chassenée lost the case, but established his reputation for creative advocacy.

Animal Attire

When guilty animals were sentenced to death, a common feature of their execution appears to have been dressing them up in human clothing. In 1386, a sow was found guilty of attacking a child. It was "dressed in men's clothes and executed on the public square."

Why Did They Do That?

During the Middle Ages life was harsh. Humans were trying to work out their place in God's scheme and were uncertain about the role of animals. Animal trials were important rituals which helped humans to exert control over the uncertainties of life and symbolically restore order to their chaotic world.

THANKSGIVING: A MOVEABLE FEAST?

Thanksgiving, or Thanksgiving Day, is an annual holiday that is held in the United States on the fourth Thursday in November, and in Canada on the second Monday in October to express thankfulness for good things. But the earliest American Thanksgiving predates the Pilgrims and, until the nineteenth century, its observance was highly erratic.

The First Thanksgiving

The event Americans associate with the first Thanksgiving took place in the autumn of 1621, when fifty colonists from Plymouth Colony threw a party to celebrate the harvest along with ninety members of the neighboring Wampanoag tribe.

However, the first Thanksgiving feast in North America was observed on May 23, 1541, at the Palo Duro Canyon in Texas, by the Spanish nobleman Francisco Vásquez de Coronado and a group of Native Americans which he called "Tejas" (from which Texas gets its name), to celebrate his expedition's discovery of food. He had traveled north from Mexico City in 1540 in search of gold. The Texas Society Daughters of the American Colonists commemorated the event in 1959 as the first Thanksgiving. To complicate matters further, the Ford County Historical Society erected a permanent cross outside Fort Dodge, Kansas, 200 miles northeast of Palo Duro Canyon, to commemorate a service of thanksgiving which Coronado is supposed to have held there on June 29, 1541, and which they claim was the first Christian service held in the interior of the continent.

A "second" Thanksgiving took place over twenty years later, on September 8, 1565, after Pedro Menéndez de Avilés landed in Florida and founded the settlement of St. Augustine (the oldest continually-inhabited city in the United States). He and his 2,000 men are believed to have shared a feast with the aboriginal peoples before attacking the nearby French colony of Fort Caroline. Menéndez de Avilés murdered everyone—men, women, and children—and hung some of the dead bodies from trees.

A "third" Thanksgiving was celebrated on April 30, 1598, near the site of San Elizario, Texas, by Don Juan de Oñate and some Manso Indians from present-day El Paso. It took place inside a large church that Oñate had ordered his men to build specially for the occasion.

A Moveable Feast

After the 1621 Thanksgiving, the event was held fairly randomly as a national celebration, and was often not held during the Fall. Individual communities would often give thanks after the harvest, but Thanksgiving did not become a national, annual event until the nineteenth century. It only became an official holiday when President Roosevelt passed a bill on November 26, 1941, to establish the fourth Thursday in November as the national Thanksgiving holiday.

Between 1777 and 1783, there were annual Thanksgiving days in December, and they weren't always to celebrate the harvest. The 1777 Thanksgiving was proclaimed by George Washington to celebrate the defeat of the British at Saratoga. In 1815, James Madison declared Thanksgiving twice after the end of the War of 1812 for "devout acknowledgments to Almighty God for His great goodness manifested in restoring to them the blessing of peace." The next Thanksgiving after that was nearly fifty years later, in April 1862.

Franklin D. Roosevelt

TULIPMANIA UNDERMINES THE DUTCH ECONOMY

The tulip was introduced to Europe in the middle of the sixteenth century and became extremely popular in Holland (which was known then as the United Provinces). The exotic flower quickly became a desirable item, and as demand grew, speculation on the tulip reached ludicrous levels, until the bubble finally burst, bankrupting thousands.

When Did Tulipmania Begin?

Tulips are thought to have originated on the steppes of western and central Asia. They then spread along the Black Sea and the Mediterranean, and they were very popular with the Ottoman Empire. In the mid-1500s, the ambassador of Austrian Emperor Ferdinand I brought a collection of tulip bulbs to Vienna and gave some to his friend, Carolus Clusius, director of the Royal Medicinal Gardens.

Tulip cultivation started in the United Provinces in the early 1590s, when Carolus Clusius sought religious sanctuary there and became the director of the botanical garden at the University of Leiden. Within a few years tulips were a coveted luxury item, and those with the brightest colors were the most sought after. Tulips infected with the Mosaic virus had flames on their petals, and these sick specimens were highly prized.

The Market Grows

By the 1620s, a single tulip bulb could fetch as much as a thousand Dutch florins, which was about six times the average annual income. By 1635 a merchant sold forty bulbs for 100,000 florins and tulips were being traded on the stock market of many Dutch towns and cities. A futures market developed, whereby traders agreed to buy and sell tulips that hadn't even been grown yet. Tulipmania was so great that thousands of people sold their possessions, even their houses and dowries, so that they could invest in tulips. Some traders were earning as much as 60,000 florins in a month (about $45,000). Tulips were sold by weight while they were still in the ground, so people could become rich just by planting bulbs and waiting for them to grow.

The Bubble Bursts

In 1637, over-supply caused the sale price of tulips to reach its peak. Prices started to fall

when traders were unable to sell at the highest prices, and panic selling began as everyone tried to offload their stock. The futures trade in tulips (known as "wind trade") had actually been banned by a state edict in 1610, but it had been impossible to enforce, so thousands of traders were committed to buying bulbs at many times higher than they were worth, or left with bulbs they couldn't sell. Within a few weeks, thousands of Dutch businessmen and ordinary people heavily exposed in the market were ruined. After the crash, the Dutch government introduced trading restrictions on the flower so that the disaster could not be repeated.

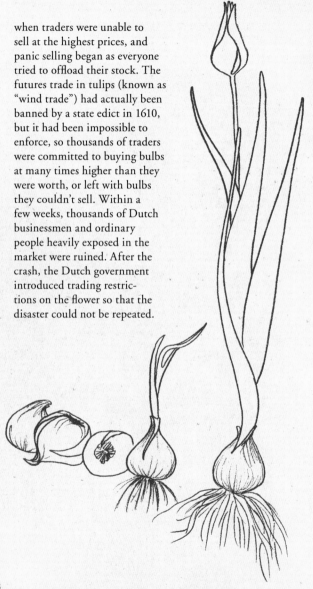

THE DOUBLE BURIAL OF SIR WALTER RALEIGH

Sir Walter Raleigh is a famous English writer, poet, and explorer who rose to prominence under the reign of Queen Elizabeth I. After being sentenced to death for treason, his body was buried at the parish church next to Westminster Abbey—but it was many years before it was reunited with his head.

What Did He Do Wrong?

Raleigh had a profound hatred of Catholicism, and was quick to express it after the Protestant Queen Elizabeth I came to the throne in 1558. He became one of her court favorites and there is a famous story (most likely a Victorian invention) that he once laid his expensive cloak over a puddle she was to walk over to keep her feet dry.

His first imprisonment was during Elizabeth's reign, after he was discovered to have secretly married one of the Queen's ladies-in-waiting, Elizabeth

("Bess") Throckmorton, who was eleven years younger than him. It took Raleigh several years to live down the scandal and to regain favor at court. However, they remained devoted to each other and had two sons, Walter and Carew.

After the Queen's death in 1603, Raleigh was implicated in a plot to overthrow the new king, James I. He was tried for treason in the converted Great Hall of Winchester Castle and imprisoned in the Tower of London until 1616. During this time, he wrote the five-volume *The Historie of the World*, about ancient Greece and Rome. After his release, he led an expedition to South America to find the lost city of El Dorado. During the expedition he attacked the Spanish settlement at San Thome, during which his son, Walter, was killed. On Sir Walter's return to England, the outraged Spanish Ambassador convinced James I to reinstate Raleigh's death sentence.

Execution

Raleigh was beheaded at Whitehall on October 29, 1618. Before placing his head on the block he asked to see the ax and observed, "This is a sharp Medicine, but it is a Physician for all Diseases."

His devoted wife, griefstricken at having lost a son and now a husband, had his head embalmed and kept it by her side in a red leather bag at all times. According to *Shepherd of the Ocean*, a biography of Raleigh by J. H. Adamson and H. F. Holland, she was in the habit of "frequently inquiring of visitors if they would like to see Sir Walter."

When she died twenty-nine years later at the age of eighty-two, the head fell into the possession of her son, Carew, who kept it until his death. On January 1, 1668, Carew was buried with the head alongside the body of Sir Walter at St. Margaret's Church, next to Westminster Abbey. It had taken fifty years for the head of Sir Walter Raleigh to reach its final resting place.

St. Margaret's Church

THE FIRST SUBMARINE INVENTED 400 YEARS AGO

The first boat known to have been sailed under water was built in 1620 by Dutchman Cornelius van Drebbel. He demonstrated it by sailing seven miles down the River Thames in front of a crowd of thousands.

Early Attempts

Records of attempts at submarine warfare date back to the writings of Herodotus (460 B.C.), Aristotle (332 B.C.), and Pliny, the elder, (A.D. 77), all of whom mention attempts to build submersibles.

The Florentine Renaissance inventor and artist Leonardo da Vinci, who died in 1519, is believed to have developed plans for an underwater warship, which he kept secret for fear of consequences.

The first serious description of a submarine was published in 1578 by British mathematician and writer William Bourne, who proposed a completely enclosed boat that could be submerged and rowed underwater. It consisted of a wooden frame surrounded with waterproof leather and hand vices to reduce the volume and make the vessel sink. Bourne never built a prototype, so it was Cornelius van Drebbel who gained the credit for the first submersible.

The submarine had twelve oars for rowing and a tube to bring air down to the vessel.

Van Drebbel's Submarine

Drebbel was born in Alkmaar in the Netherlands in 1572, the son of a wealthy farmer. Despite his lack of a university education, he was an accomplished engraver and inventor. He designed a water-supply system for his hometown, and in 1598 he patented a perpetual motion device that caught the attention of King James I of England, who invited him to court to preside over a royal fireworks display.

It would be another fourteen years before he devoted himself to the construction of a submarine, while in the employ of the British Navy. Drebbel's submarine was similar in design to Bourne's, with greased leather stretched over a wooden frame serving as the outer hull. It was propelled by a bank of twelve oars that poked out of the sides, through holes made watertight with leather gaskets. Drebbel performed exhaustive trials with the vessel between 1620 and 1624 in the River Thames in London and suc-ceeded in reaching a depth of fifteen feet. Its air supply came from snorkel air tubes attached to floats on the surface, which allowed the submariners to stay submerged for several hours.

After the success of his prototype he built two bigger versions which could travel underwater from Westminster to Greenwich and back. However, the British Navy was more interested in his development of explosives and never used his submarine, despite the fact that King James I rode in one of them without coming to any harm as thousands of Londoners lined the bank of the Thames to marvel at the spectacle.

It is said that Drebbel attempted to develop an air-conditioning system that allowed the crew to stay submerged for longer. He also discovered how to make oxygen from heating saltpeter. Regrettably for future generations, Drebbel was so secretive that he left no account of his submarine, not even a drawing.

MANHATTAN ISLAND SOLD FOR TWENTY-FOUR DOLLARS

On the east coast of the United States is an island of approximately twenty square miles, measuring thirteen miles long and 2.3 miles across at its widest point. It is the financial and commercial center of the United States and represents some of the most expensive real estate on the planet. Nearly 400 years ago, local Indians sold this property—Manhattan Island—in exchange for $24 of merchandise.

Where Does the Name Come From?

The name Manhattan derives from the word Manna-hata, the European name for the Native American people who lived there (and who today are believed to have been the Lenape tribe, an Algonquian aboriginal American people also called the "Delaware"). The word appears in the 1609 logbook of Robert Juet, who was an officer on board the *Half Moon*, owned by the Dutch West India Company. The ship was tasked with a secret mission to discover a Northwest Passage to China. It reached Upper New York Bay on September 11, 1609, and anchored off the northern tip of Manhattan. The ship's captain, Henry Hudson, named the river up which he had just sailed the Mauritius River, after Holland's Lord Lieutenant, Maurits. It was later renamed the Hudson River.

New Amsterdam

The fortress town of New Amsterdam on Manhattan Island was founded in 1625 by the director of the Dutch West India Company, Willem Verhulst, who selected Manhattan as the best place to establish

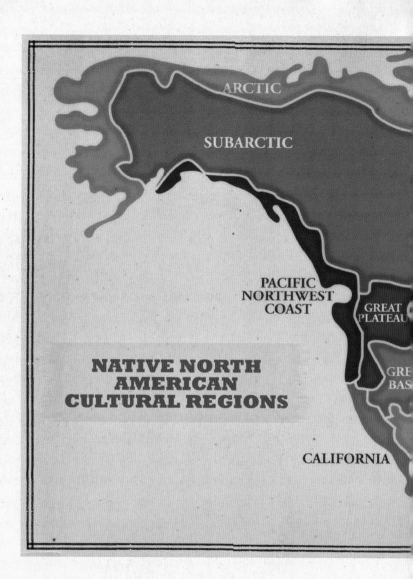

ARCTIC

SUBARCTIC

PACIFIC
NORTHWEST
COAST

GREAT
PLATEAU

GRE
BAS

NATIVE NORTH
AMERICAN
CULTURAL REGIONS

CALIFORNIA

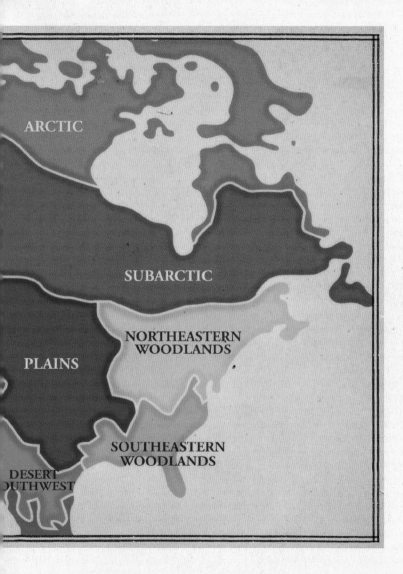

ARCTIC

SUBARCTIC

NORTHEASTERN
WOODLANDS

PLAINS

SOUTHEASTERN
WOODLANDS

DESERT
SOUTHWEST

After The Purchase Of Manhatan Island by Alfred Frederick

the first permanent European settlement in what was later to become part of New York City.

Military engineer and surveyor Cryn Fredericksz van Lobbrecht laid out a citadel on the island with Fort New Amsterdam as its centerpiece.

Manhattan Sold

In 1626 Verhulst's successor, Peter Minuit, purchased the island from the Lenape for 60 guilders worth of goods such as cloth, furs, and tools. The value of these items equated to about $24, which is the equivalent of $500 to $700 in today's currency.

A record of the sale appears in *New World*, a book written by Johannes de Laet, the Director of the Dutch West India Company, and published in 1630: "another fort [New Amsterdam] of greater importance at the mouth of the same North River, upon an island which our people call Manhattas or Manhattans Island, because of this nation of Indians happened to possess the same, and by them it has been sold to the company."

The Lenape, like many Native Americans, had no concept of land ownership; they believed that land could no more be owned than could the air, water, or sunlight. They lived in peace with European settlers and they no doubt believed that they had accepted the trade goods as a token of appreciation for sharing the land. When they later tried to forcefully reclaim the land, the settlers built a wall to keep them out. That wall later became Wall Street, the future location of the New York Stock Exchange.

Wall Street

THE MURDERER FROM THE MAYFLOWER

On September 6, 1620, the *Mayflower* left Plymouth, England and sailed across the Atlantic carrying the first Pilgrims. It also carried a man who would become the first person to be convicted of murder in the United States. His name was John Billington.

Billington was not one of the separatist Puritans, the so-called "Saints." Rather, he belonged to the group of passengers who became known as the "Strangers." He is thought to have joined the voyage to escape from his debts in England. He sailed with his wife Elinor and his teenage sons John, Jr. and Francis.

Trouble at Sea

The disruptiveness of the Billington family was apparent during the voyage. Young Francis Billington nearly blew up the *Mayflower* by firing his father's musket near an open barrel of gunpowder while the ship was docked in Provincetown Harbor. If the

barrel had ignited the whole ship would have been destroyed, along with most of the Pilgrims.

According to historian George F. Willison, John was "unquestionably one of those mixed up in the mutiny on the *Mayflower*," which nearly erupted when some passengers challenged the governing authority in their new land. The mutiny was pre-empted by the drafting of the Mayflower Compact, for which Billington was one of the signatories.

Trouble on Land

Shortly after the pilgrims arrived at Plymouth, which would later become part of Massachusetts, John Billington was charged with "contempt of the Captain's [Myles Standish] lawful command with opprobrious speeches," and was sentenced to have his neck and heels tied together, "but upon humbling himself and craving pardon, and it being the first offence" he was forgiven.

First Winter

During the typhus epidemic that tore through the settler's population during the first winter at Plymouth, the Billingtons were the only family who did not lose one of its members. Elinor was one of only five adult women to survive the first winter, and one of only four who was still alive at the 1621 Thanksgiving.

John and his two sons soon became notorious for their exploits in the colony. Francis set off to discover a new ocean and discovered a lake behind the town. He named it the Billington Sea, which it is still called today. John, Jr. wandered off in May 1621, and ended up living for a month with the Nauset Indians in Cape Cod, before he was returned.

Oldham-Lyford Scandal

In 1624, John Billington was implicated in the Oldham-Lyford scandal, a failed revolt against the Plymouth colony, in which disparaging letters were secretly sent to England. There wasn't enough evidence to convict Billington, who believed he was a scapegoat, and the matter was dropped.

America's First Murder

Ten years after arriving in Plymouth, John Billington got into a quarrel with John Newcomen and shot him with a musket. He was tried and found guilty "by plain and notorious evidence," and on September 30, 1630, he became the first Englishman to be hanged in New England.

CZAR PETER THE GREAT'S TAX ON BEARDS

Peter the Great was one of the greatest leaders that Russia has ever seen. He transformed his inward-looking, isolated country by modernizing its economy and building a superior army and navy. He opened up trade routes and expanded his empire, but his reforms didn't come cheap; they were paid for by his people, who were directly taxed on everything from beards to beehives.

Turbulent Childhood

Born on May 30, 1672, Peter Romanov was the youngest son of Czar Alexei Mikhailovich by his second wife, Natalya Naryshkin. His childhood was overshadowed by power struggles for the throne. When his father died in 1676, Peter's older brother, Feodor III, ruled until his death six years later. After a bloody revolution was fought to decide whether Peter or his mentally challenged brother, Ivan V, should take power, the brothers shared power, but ten-year-old Peter was sent away by his older sister, Sophia, so she could become regent.

Peter Comes of Age

Just as Peter approached the age where he could take power, Sophia attempted a coup, which Peter and his supporters quelled. When Ivan V died, Peter assumed sole control of Russia. He immediately set about modernizing the country, and spent the rest of his life pursuing this goal.

European Tour

Before making sweeping changes, Peter did what any great leader would do: he listened

Peter the Great

and learned. He spent two years on a grand tour of Europe, but he didn't just go hunting and dining with other heads of state; he recruited hundreds of Western engineers, miners, shipbuilders, architects, and other skilled workers and brought their expertise to Russia. He also learned dentistry, seamanship, and shipbuilding, and used this knowledge on his return to Russia to build a formidable modern navy.

Domestic Reforms

Peter built the city of St. Petersburg at a great human cost, earning the city the nickname "the city built on bones." He transformed the educational system, opened up trade routes, and imported many Western goods. He also instructed his noblemen to wear modern clothes rather than their archly conservative Oriental costumes, and to cut off their beards. On April 26, 1698, he assembled his chief officials and personally clipped off their beards and moustaches.

All men, except peasants and priests, had to pay an annual beard tax and wear a medal that said, "Beards are a ridiculous ornament." He set up a committee specifically to devise new ways of taxing the people. Taxes were raised on everything from beehives, boots, and candles to chimneys, hats, horses, and even drinking water.

BRITAIN'S TWELVE-DAY SLEEP

On Wednesday, September 2, 1752, the inhabitants of Britain and the colonies went to bed that evening as usual, but woke up twelve days later. Millions of people lost nearly a fortnight of their lives. This curious phenomenon was not the result of a national attack of narcolepsy; it was the consequence of an act of Parliament that had been passed the previous year.

Let's Blame Julius Caesar

Prior to that September evening, the British were still using a calendar that had been invented by Julius Caesar in 45 B.C. The "Julian" calendar had eleven months of thirty or thirty-one days, and one month, February, with twenty-eight days (extended to twenty-nine days every fourth year). As calendars went it was quite accurate, losing only about 11½ minutes every year, but after nearly 1,800 years this added up to a sizeable discrepancy.

Julius Caesar

Next, Let's Ignore the Pope

By the end of the sixteenth century the Julian calendar was ten days behind the solar calendar, so in 1582 Pope Gregory XIII advanced the calendar by ten days and decreed that century years would not be counted as leap years unless they were divisible by four. However, many Protestant countries, such as England, ignored his papal bull. It was a full seventy years before the British came to their senses and issued the British Calendar Act of 1751, which decreed that Wednesday, September 2, 1752 would be followed by Thursday, September 14.

Pope Gregory XIII

The Rest of Europe Plays Catch-up

Although Catholic countries such as France and Spain had been enjoying the benefits of the Gregorian calendar since 1582, some countries waited even longer than England to adopt it. Russia switched after the revolution in 1918, and Greece waited until 1923.

Does Anyone Still Use the Lunar Calendar?

The Muslim calendar is the only lunar calendar being used today. The months are not fixed to the seasons, so, for example, Ramadan can fall on any day of the year as measured by the Gregorian calendar. The Hebrew calendar is semi-lunar, in that it has twelve twenty-nine- and thirty-day months, resulting in an extra month seven times every nineteen years.

The French Revolutionary Calendar

October 5, 1793 saw another attempt to change the calendar when the French Revolutionary Convention decreed that there would be twelve months of thirty days each and that weeks would be abolished. Instead, each month would be split into three groups of ten, with every tenth day being a day of rest. The remaining five days (called *sans-culottides*) were declared feast days. This calendar was straightforward, but it died with the Revolution.

THE HAT THAT CAUSED A RIOT

The top hat was the epitome of Victorian elegance and dominated the nineteenth century. Men would not be seen in public without one, whether they were conducting business, pleasure, or attending a formal occasion. Fashion even dictated that men wear gray top hats for daytime, although black was allowable at any time. However, on its first outing this pillar of social decorum didn't just turn heads, it caused a riot.

Haberdasher Cuts a Dash

John Hetherington was a London haberdasher during the late eighteenth century. He is thought to have developed the top hat in 1797 by making modifications to the similar riding hat, which was round, cylindrical, and flat. He merely increased the height and size of the brim and he used shiny silk instead of the traditional beaver fur to create his imposing new headwear. His biggest mistake was wearing it in public.

Breach of the Peace

The first time John Hetherington wore his new hat in public,
women screamed and fainted,
men booed, dogs yelped, and a
large crowd formed around him.
An errand boy was trampled
by the mob and broke his arm.
The disruption seems to have
been caused by a combination
of the hat's height and shini-
ness. Hetherington was brought
before a court and charged with
disturbing the peace by "appearing on the public highway
wearing upon his head a tall
structure having a shining luster
and calculated to frighten timid
people." He was found guilty
and fined £50, a considerable
amount in those days, and
a law was passed forbidding
people from wearing top hats.

Prince Albert to the Rescue

Initially, society was resistant to
Hetherington's silk topper, and
many gentlemen continued to
favor beaver hats. Top hats eventually became popular around
1820, when they were very com-
monly worn by men for affairs of
business and pleasure, but they
were still made from stiffened
beaver fur. Silk toppers finally
became fashionable in the 1850s
after Prince Albert started wearing top hats made of "hatter's
plush" (a fine coarse-woven silk).

PLANTING OF THE FIRST TAMPA BAY GRAPEFRUIT TREE

A French count planted the first Florida grapefruit tree as a novelty in 1823. He couldn't have foreseen that two hundred years later his handful of seeds would grow into a multi-million-dollar business producing about one-third of the world's grapefruit and about three-quarters of the United States' supply.

A Brief History of the Grapefruit

The story of the grapefruit begins in southeastern China and Japan with its nearest relative, the shaddock, or pummelo. This large tree has a round top and huge ovate leaves. It blossoms into bunches of crisp white flowers and its fruit is the largest of all the citrus trees. The shaddock was named for Captain Shaddock, an English ship commander of an East Indian ship who brought the seeds of the large fruit from China to Barbados during the seventeenth century.

The shaddock thrived in the warm climate of Barbados. Then, in 1750, the Reverend Griffith Hughes wrote about the "forbidden fruit" of Barbados. His description of a "smaller shaddock" suggests that he had observed a completely new fruit, a mutant variation of the shaddock: the grapefruit.

By 1789 Patrick Browne reported that the "forbidden fruit" was also growing in Jamaica. In 1814, John Lunan described it for the first time as a "grapefruit" (possibly because clusters of the fruit resemble grapes) and as "a variety

of the shaddock, but the fruit is much smaller, having a thin, tough, smooth, pale yellow rind."

Count Odette Philippe

The grapefruit continued to spread around the West Indies, and it was from the Bahamas that Count Odette Philippe took some seeds to plant around his homestead at Safety Harbor near Tampa, Florida in 1823. Born in Lyon, France, Odette lived in the Bahamas only because he had been banished there by the British. He had been a surgeon in Napoleon's army and became a prisoner of war at the Battle of Trafalgar.

When the trees fruited, the Count was able to give seeds to his neighbors, who started growing grapefruit trees as a novelty rather than for their fruit. Eating the fruit was slow to catch on and one American gardening encyclopedia called it "thick-skinned and worthless."

The First Nursery

By 1840, the grapefruit had grown in popularity, but it wasn't until 1870 that the first grapefruit nursery was established by John A. MacDonald in Orange County, Florida. Fifteen years later Florida's first shipment of grapefruits reached New York and Philadelphia, establishing Florida as a major commercial grapefruit center.

A Lucky Escape

Florida's grapefruit industry owes its existence today to three men: a seventeenth-century seadog, a French Count, and a British Admiral. If Horatio Nelson had lost the historical sea battle which took place off the coast of Spain on October 21, 1805, Count Odette Philippe and his small yellow fruit would never have become acquainted.

DEAD MAN PRESIDES OVER UNIVERSITY COLLEGE LONDON MEETINGS

The British philosopher Jeremy Bentham was a leading theorist in Anglo-American philosophy of law and the leading exponent of utilitarianism. When he died in 1832, he left his entire estate to the University College London on condition that his body would be wheeled into board meetings. His dying wishes are still being observed today, nearly two centuries later.

Jeremy Bentham

Life and Work

Born into a wealthy Tory family, Jeremy Bentham was educated at Westminster School and Queen's College, Oxford. After training as a lawyer he was called to the bar in 1769. Because of his family's wealth he was able to devote his time to study and writing. According to his contemporary, William Hazlitt, "Bentham has lived for the last forty years in a house in Westminster . . . like an anchorite in a cell, reducing law to a system, and the mind of man to a machine."

In 1789 Bentham published his most famous work, *Introduction to the Principles of Morals*, which separates the two root drives of human essence into categories of pleasure and pain, and establishes the principles of utilitarianism. The theory approves of an action if it has an overall tendency to promote the greatest amount of happiness. Happiness is identified with pleasure and the absence of pain.

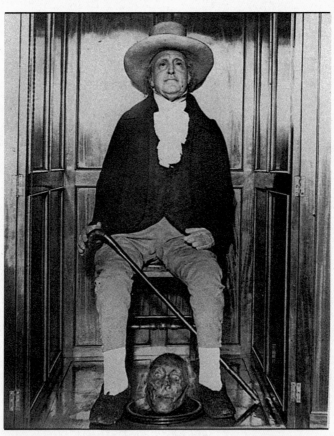

Founding of the University of London

Bentham is often credited with being the founder of the University of London, a forerunner of University College London (UCL). He was in his late seventies when UCL opened in 1826, and while he didn't play an active role in its founding, his egalitarian spirit and beliefs would certainly have influenced its creation. He strongly believed that education should be made widely available, regardless of wealth, social status or religious beliefs. UCL was the first British university to admit students without regard to race and religious or political beliefs.

Life After Death

Bentham died on June 6, 1832. As instructed in his will, his body was embalmed, dressed, and placed on display in a glass cabinet in the hallways of UCL. It is still there today, sitting on a chair and dressed in a black jacket, fawn breeches, and a straw-colored wide-brimmed hat, holding his stick, "Dapple." He is wheeled in to preside over the annual meeting of university administrators. As well as donating his estate to UCL, Bentham also left tens of thousands of pages of unpublished papers that are still being catalogued and studied.

The polished wood-paneled cabinet that holds his body was initially called his "Auto-Icon," and today it sits at the end of the South Cloisters in the main building of the college. When he appears at Council meetings, Bentham is listed on the minutes as "present but not voting."

Student Pranks

Bentham's body has always had a wax head, as his real head was damaged during the embalming process. The real head was kept in the case for many years, but students kept stealing it, so it is now locked away in a vault elsewhere on the premises.

THE TRAGEDY OF HORACE WELLS

Hartford dentist Horace Wells is a forgotten pioneer in the history of dentistry and anesthesia. He was the first person to recognize how nitrous oxide, or "laughing gas," could be used in surgical medicine to reduce the suffering of patients. However, after his assistant stole his techniques, he used his anesthesia research to assist in his own painless suicide.

Laughing Gas Show

On December 10, 1844, Horace and his wife Elizabeth went to a stage-show performed by "Professor" Gardner Quincy Colton. During the show several volunteers were invited to inhale laughing gas and their subsequent hilarious antics were intended to amuse the audience. On this occasion one of the participants, a store-clerk named Sam Cooley, ran into the audience chasing an imaginary enemy. Then he returned to his seat to discover that he had lacerated his leg during the chase, although he felt no pain until the effects of the gas had worn off.

Horace the Human Guinea Pig

Horace Wells immediately recognized the surgical applications of the gas, and asked Colton to come to his surgery so that they could perform a tooth extraction using nitrous oxide. Wells had one of his colleagues remove a troublesome wisdom tooth, after Colton, with much persuasion from Wells, had administered enough gas to make him unconscious. The operation was a resounding success. The two men then collaborated to perform pain-free operations on several other patients. Wells used an animal bladder and a wooden tube to administer the gas and put his patients to sleep; the technique was crude but effective and seemed complication-free.

Public Humiliation

After performing over a dozen extractions, Wells's assistant, William Morton, encouraged him to give a public lecture to demonstrate his technique at Massachusetts General Hospital. However, the demonstration didn't go as planned. Wells, writing in the *Hartford Courant* on December 9, 1846, described the events:

"A large number of students, with several physicians, met to see the operation performed— one of their number to be the patient. Unfortunately for the experiment, the gasbag was by mistake withdrawn much too soon, and he was but partially under its influence when the tooth was extracted. He testified that he experienced some pain, but not as much as usually attends the operation. As there was no other patient present, that the experiment might be repeated, and as several expressed their opinion that it was a humbug affair (which in fact was all the thanks I got for this gratuitous service) I accordingly left the next morning for home."

Betrayal and Suicide

Wells was booed out of the lecture hall. Embarrassed and humiliated, he returned to

Hartford and sold his practice. His failure was compounded when he discovered that Morton had developed ether-based anesthesia and was using it at Massachusetts General Hospital with great success.

After a spell in France, where he failed to revive his career, he moved to New York where his experiments with chloroform made him increasingly unhinged. After attacking two prostitutes with sulfuric acid, he was sent to prison, where he committed suicide by cutting a large artery in his leg, after inhaling chloroform to numb the pain.

WHEN NIAGARA FALLS STOPPED FALLING

On Tuesday, March 30, 1848, residents who lived close to Niagara Falls woke up to an eerie silence. The thundering roar of water that formed the backdrop to their daily lives was absent. The night before, the flow of water had reduced to a trickle and stayed that way for the next thirty hours. It is the only time in recorded history that the Horseshoe Falls, the largest of the three falls, fell silent.

Why Did It Stop Flowing?

The winter of 1847-1848 had not been unusually cold and on March 29 the weather was clear, with an air temperature of nearly 45 degrees Fahrenheit. However, for several days before the event, a gale-force wind had been blowing from the southwest over Lake Erie. This caused a jam of ice at the mouth of the Niagara River that stopped the water from flowing. The river didn't freeze solid—it was dammed up.

Crowds Gather Along the Banks of the River

On Tuesday morning more than 5,000 people gathered to view the empty rocks over which, hours earlier, millions of cubic feet of water had tumbled every minute. All the factories further downriver that relied on water for their power were forced to close. Several people walked onto the empty riverbed and salvaged souvenirs that had been inaccessible for centuries, including bayonets, muskets, tomahawks, and other artifacts from the War of 1812. A squad of U.S. Calvary rode on the riverbed and a group of workers blasted away an outcrop of rocks that had been hazardous to the *Maid of the Mist* boat that had been giving visitors a close-up view of the Falls.

The End of the World?

Throughout Tuesday and the next day the deafening silence continued and residents became increasingly anxious that it presaged an impending disaster. A special church service was held on the Wednesday, attended by thousands of people. Finally that evening the wind over Lake Erie shifted and the temperature rose, causing the ice dam to break up. Residents at the Falls heard a deep rumbling sound that signaled the water was returning.

Could Horseshoe Falls Be Silenced Again?

Because an ice boom has been placed in Lake Erie to protect water intakes for nearby hydroelectric power stations, the Falls cannot be silenced again by natural causes.

On six reported occasions (1883, 1896, 1904, 1909, 1936, and 1947), the water flow over the smaller American Falls has been choked-up by ice, which has stopped it from falling. On two other occasions water flow was stopped artificially: In 1953, water was kept from flowing over part of the Horseshoe Falls by the building of coffer dams, so that engineers could perform repair work to slow down erosion. In 1969, the U.S. Army used coffer dams to reduce the water rate of the American Falls to a trickle. This allowed them to study the rocks and to explore the feasibility of removing the rocks at the bottom, which they concluded would be too expensive.

ABE LINCOLN SCORES FIFTY-CENTS' WORTH OF COCAINE

On October 12, 1860, Abraham Lincoln walked into the Corneau & Diller drug store in Springfield, Illinois, and purchased fifty-cents' worth of cocaine. The alkaloid had only been isolated from the coca plant five years earlier, and had only been named "cocaine" by Albert Nieman the year before. This makes Abe Lincoln one of the first Americans to use this brand-new drug.

The Origins of Cocaine

The South American natives have smoked, chewed, and swallowed coca leaves for centuries. The leaves were also used as a local anesthetic. European explorers returned from the New World with stories of coca, but medicinal coca products didn't become popular until the nineteenth century. Coca wines were introduced in France in the 1860s and spread to the rest of the world.

How Do We Know He Bought It?

In the 1930s, Harry E. Pratt was researching for his book, *The Personal Finances of Abraham Lincoln*, which was published in 1943. He studied the order book of Corneau & Diller and found a fifty-cent purchase of cocaine on October 12, 1860. Other historians have studied the earlier order books and have discovered three sales to the Lincoln household of another powerful medicine: ten cents on April 29 and July 25, 1853, and sixty cents on March 22, 1854. The medicine was paregoric, or camphorated opium tincture, known for its antidiarrheal and analgesic properties. Its main ingredient was morphine. However, as author Walter Olesky points out, "Little was then known about the drug's side effects. For Mary Lincoln the side effects were depression, mood swings, and hallucinations."

Mr. and Mrs. Lincoln's Depression

It is well documented that Abe and his wife, Mary, both suffered from profound depression. As a young man Lincoln often talked about suicide and one of his colleagues, Henry Whitney declared, "No element of Mr. Lincoln's character was so marked, obvious and ingrained as his mysterious and profound melancholy." His law partner, William Herndon, said, "His melancholy dripped from him as he walked." After her husband's assassination Mary Lincoln was briefly committed to an asylum by her son, for a history of erratic behavior. The fact that she outlived her husband and three of her four sons could not have helped her mental health.

Cocaine became a popular treatment for a host of mental and medical diseases, and melancholy was one of them. It was considered a "brain tonic" and increasingly became viewed as a cure-all.

Lincoln Is Elected President

A month after purchasing his cocaine, Abraham Lincoln became the sixteenth President of the United States and, according to Joshua Wolf Shenk, in *Lincoln's Melancholy*, "the troughs of despair became deeper, and the need for creative response became all the more intense." It is not known whether he continued to use cocaine, since no other records of such purchases survive.

Abraham Lincoln's inauguration March 4, 1861.

THE BIRTH OF THE FIVE-CENT BILL

Today, the idea of a bill worth a nickel seems incongruous, but during the U.S. Civil War metal was in short supply and so, between 1862 and 1876, low-denomination paper money was issued. These curious bills were known as fractional currency and many examples survive today.

The Civil War Drags On

Many people thought that the Civil War would be quick, but as it dragged on they started feeling insecure about their money and began hoarding their silver and gold coins. The government restricted production of new copper coinage because it needed the metal for weapons and machinery, so coins became increasingly hard to find. To solve this problem, Congress was obliged to pass a law permitting the use of postage stamps as legal tender.

A Sticky Mess

The Post Office didn't like selling postage stamps for currency, and refused to replace dirty or damaged ones. Stamps aren't designed to be passed around from person to person and they were easily lost. One man, John Gault, invented a way of protecting stamps by encasing them between two round pieces of thin brass. The top shell had a window, so the denomination of the stamp inside could be seen. These were known as "encased postage stamps."

Stamp Crisis

Inevitably, the increased demand for postage stamps meant that they, too, ran out, so there were no stamps for mailing letters. Eventually, General F. E. Spinner, the U.S. Treasurer, convinced the government to produce fractional currency. On July 17, 1862, President Lincoln approved the Postage Currency Act that authorized an issue of five-, ten-, twenty-five-, and fifty-cent bills, and they started being used on August 21 of that year. These bills were much smaller than the currency we are familiar with today. They looked like postage stamps and for the first few months of production they even had perforations. Later versions were produced in plain sheets and the straight edges were cut to size with scissors. The first issues were never legal tender, but they could be collected and exchanged for notes in lots of $5.

This early "postage currency" was easy to counterfeit, so subsequent fractional currency notes were made more colorful and had printing on both sides. These curious bills continued to be produced until February 15, 1876.

Shinplasters

The bills gained the nickname "shinplasters," because soldiers were paid in fractional currency and often stuffed the bills into their boots to keep out the cold.

THE MYSTERY OF THE LOST CIGARS

On the morning of September 13, 1862, at the height of the American Civil War, three Union soldiers were resting with their unit in a clover field two miles south of Frederick, Maryland. Suddenly, one of them spotted a paper package lying in the grass. Inside, they found three small cigars and a two-page letter written by Confederate General Robert E. Lee, detailing the battle strategy for his Maryland campaign. How these vital plans arrived at where they were found has been the subject of much debate, but the Union discovery of Special Orders No. 191, the name given to Lee's letter, was a major turning point in the war.

The Discovery

The three resting soldiers were First Sergeant John M. Bloss, Corporal Barton Warren Mitchell, and Private David Bur Vance of the Union's 27th Indiana Infantry. Initially, they were unsure whether the orders lying in the grass were genuine or a *ruse de guerre*, but they had the good sense to inform their unit commander, Captain Peter Kop. The letter passed quickly up the chain of command until it was couriered to General George B. McClellan, the commander of the Army of the Potomac. It arrived by midday. McClellan was satisfied that the orders were genuine, and that they offered him vital information. His intelligence reports had suggested that Lee had divided his forces, and Lee's letter confirmed it. He is said to have exclaimed, "Now I know what to do!" He then remarked to one of his men, "Here is a paper with which, if I cannot whip Bobby Lee, I will be willing to go home."

What Did the Orders Say?

Dated September 9, 1862, addressed to Major General D. H. Hill, and signed by R. H. Chilton, Assistant Adjutant-General to General Lee, the document contained detailed instructions for placing all of Lee's units. For example: "General McLaws with his own division and that of General R. H. Anderson, will follow General Longstreet; on reaching Middletown he will take the route to Harper's Ferry, and by Friday morning possess himself of the Maryland Heights and endeavor to capture the enemy at Harper's Ferry and vicinity."

How Did the Orders End Up in the Clover Field?

It has never been proved conclusively whether the orders were dropped in the field by accident or placed there on purpose. Lee claimed afterwards that he could not comprehend how the orders could have been lost "as couriers were always required to bring receipt to show that written orders were safely and surely delivered."

It has been established that General Hill received a separate copy of the orders, and that the document found in the field was a duplicate. Historian Wilbur D. Jones quotes General Thomas L. Rosser, an eyewitness to the events which preceded the loss: "It was one of Jackson's staff, who was a smoker; that when it was handed to him to deliver, he said, 'O, we have that order,' and so, carelessly, wrapped it around his cigars, placed it in his pocket, and lost it in that shape." Jones believes the alleged culprit is Henry Kyd Douglas: "he was Jackson's trusted courier; he smoked cigars; and his subsequent behavior raises a level of suspicion."

Why Was It a Major Turning Point?

The information contained in the orders encouraged McClellan to pursue Lee's divided army and force a clash four days later at the Battle of Antietam, which Lee lost, and from which the South never fully recovered. The repercussions of that defeat were significant: President Abraham Lincoln gained the necessary political capital to sign the Emancipation Proclamation, and powerful European nations refused to recognize the Confederacy. After his defeat, Lee withdrew his forces to Virginia, which changed the course of the war and ultimately led to the defeat of the Confederacy.

Battle of Antietam

U.S. PRESIDENT KILLED BY HIS DOCTORS

On June 30, 1882, Charles Guiteau, the man who shot U.S. President James Garfield, argued at his trial that he did not kill the president and that the president's doctors were responsible for his death. Guiteau was sentenced to death and hanged, but what really happened during the days that followed Garfield's shooting is a testament to medical ineptitude.

When Did He Shoot the President?

Guiteau shot the president with two bullets on the morning of July 2, 1881, in the waiting room of the Baltimore and Potomac railroad depot. He was a religious fanatic who gave his motive as wishing "to unite the Republican Party and save the Republic." He had also sought an ambassadorship from Garfield's administration but had been repeatedly turned down. He gave himself up to the police instantly. In fact, he had even pre-booked a hackney cab to take him to jail, to avoid being attacked by an angry mob.

Charles Guiteau

Where Was the President Injured?

One bullet grazed the president's arm and the other lodged somewhere in his body. He was rushed to the White House for the best emergency treatment in the country, but the next ten weeks proved a textbook case of medical negligence and incompetence.

An Expert Opinion

Garfield's first doctor, Willard Bliss, put his unsterilized finger into the wound, then inserted a probe to locate the bullet. He did so much damage that physicians who arrived later discovered a much enlarged wound and wrongly concluded that the bullet had entered the liver.

A Second and Third Opinion

Next, two senior surgeons rummaged around the wound with unwashed fingers and actually punctured the liver. They concluded that the president would be dead within twenty-four hours.

Enter the Inventor

Even Alexander Graham Bell was called in, and he devised a crude metal detector to find the bullet. Surgeons operated when Bell announced he had discovered the bullet, when in fact he had unwittingly detected the metal spring under the mattress. (Coil-spring mattresses were a rare luxury in those days, and few people had even heard of them, so it is little wonder that Bell was so easily misled.)

A Hopeless Cause

By now the wound was deep and massively infected. After eighty days of this torture Garfield's wound had grown from three inches to twenty. He finally suffered a fatal heart attack and died on September 19. The incompetent surgeons incorrectly blamed death on the rupturing of a blood vessel in his stomach.

At the autopsy, the bullet was discovered in a relatively harmless position, well away from his spine. Garfield would have survived if the doctors had only left him alone.

THE THIRTY-EIGHT-MINUTE WAR

On the morning of August 27, 1896, England defeated Zanzibar in a war that lasted just thirty-eight minutes. Although listed by the *Guinness Book of Records* as the shortest war in history, 600 people were killed in the conflict.

What Caused the War?

The war was fought over the succession of Zanzibar, a British protectorate on the east coast of Africa, after the death of Sultan Hamad bin Thuwaini two days earlier. Sir Basil Cave, the British Consul, declared that Hamad's cousin, Hamoud bin Muhammed, would succeed him, but this was disputed by Khaled bin Bargash, another one of the deceased sultan's cousins. He was the eldest son of the second Sultan of Zanzibar, Sayyid Barghash bin Said Al-Busaid, and therefore believed that his claim to the throne was the strongest.

Khaled Storms the Palace

Khaled took control of the royal palace, Beit el Sahel, with an army of 2,800 men and barricaded himself inside. He raised the Zanzibar flag and proclaimed himself the rightful sultan. His supporters also seized the sultan's armed yacht, *Glasgow*, which was anchored in the harbor.

Sultan's harem after the bombardment

British Warships Prepare

The British authorities refused to recognize Khaled's claim. Sultan Hamad had willingly cooperated with the British colonial administration and they felt that Hamoud would be easier to deal with than his cousin, Khaled. Therefore, three British warships anchored in the town's harbor in front of the palace and prepared themselves for war, while marines led by General Lloyd Mathews began to evacuate Europeans to the British Consulate. That night tensions rose, and in the morning two more warships arrived in the harbor.

There were now five ships pointing their guns at the royal palace. Cave issued Khaled with an ultimatum: He had until 9:00 A.M. to vacate the palace or the fleet would open fire.

No Negotiations

At 8:00 A.M. Khaled requested negotiations with the British through a U.S. representative, but his request was refused. At 9:02 A.M. the British fleet started shelling the palace and other strategic locations in the city. At 9:40 A.M., with the palace in ruins, the *Glasgow* sunk, and 500 of his men killed (as well as 100 British), Khaled surrendered and fled to the German consulate where he was given asylum.

The British demanded that the Germans hand over Khaled but he fled to Dar es Salaam in Tanzania, where he was captured by the British twenty years later. He was eventually allowed to live in Mombasa, Kenya, where he died in 1927.

The End of Slavery

After Hamoud took power, the British pressured him to stop Zanzibar's role as a center for the eastern slave trade that had begun under Omani rule two hundred years earlier. He was decorated by Queen Victoria for banning slavery and freeing the slaves of Zanzibar.

NEW ZEALAND FARMER FLIES BEFORE THE WRIGHT BROTHERS

On December 13, 1903, two self-taught engineers made history with a twelve-second flight above the beaches of Kitty Hawk, North Carolina. Wilbur and Orville Wright gained the credit for making the first flight in a heavier-than-air flying machine, but their feat was actually predated by a farmer in the small, close-knit, farming settlement of Waitohi in New Zealand. The name of this remarkable reclusive genius was Richard Pearse.

The Forgotten Pioneer

Little is known about Richard Pearse's early life. He was born in 1877 and received only a primary school education. He spent his adult life dedicated to his inventions, which included various types of farm machinery. He had a reputation for being a mad inventor and experienced religious opposition to his aircraft, so he worked in secret, designing and building everything single-handedly. His achievements are remarkable considering that he worked alone, while the Wright brothers had a team of skilled engineers and later enjoyed government funding.

Richard Pearse

Pearse's Plane

Pearse's monoplane had a wingspan of about 250 feet and tricycle landing gear, as well as a sophisticated method of controlling the lift: ailerons, or hinged control surfaces attached to the trailing edge of the wing which are used in modern airplanes, and are vastly superior to the wing warping system used by the Wright brothers. Pearse's propeller was much cruder than theirs, but unlike the Wrights he welded it directly onto the crankshaft, eliminating the need for a flywheel and saving significant weight.

First Flight

Pearse flew many times before the Wright brothers, and may have been airborne as early as 1901, but most of his flights took place in secret, hidden from view by fifteen-foot-high gorse hedges. He never publicized his invention, took no photographs, and none of his records remain.

Pearse often used a neighbor's paddock as a runway, and during wet conditions he used the road that ran past the local school. According to corroborated eyewitness accounts from twenty-one men and women in the 1950s who had been school children at the turn of the century, he flew on March 31, 1902. He traveled around 350 yards in a straight line and with minimal control. He flew several times the following year and on May 11, 1903, after taking off from the side of the Opihi River, he made a 1,000-yard flight, including banking turns to the right and the left; he flew over the head of one local eyewitness, Arthur Tozer, and landed on the riverbed after the engine overheated.

Posthumous Discovery

Soon afterwards, with the Wright brothers taking all the credit, Pearse lost interest in aviation and became increasingly reclusive, dying an old man in a mental hospital in 1953. After his death, a partially-built, folding-wing propeller-driven aircraft was discovered in his garage. It had a tiltable engine and was designed to take off and land almost vertically. It was years ahead of its time. A search of the Opihi riverbed uncovered the remains of his earlier plane, including engine cylinders, a cast-iron piston, and a propeller.

ARCHDUKE FRANZ FERDINAND'S NEAR-BUNGLED ASSASSINATION

On June 28, 1914, the heir presumptive to the Austro-Hungarian throne, Archduke Franz Ferdinand, and his wife Sophie were killed in Sarajevo by Gavrilo Princip. The event, known as the Assassination in Sarajevo, is one of the most famous assassinations in history, as it helped to trigger World War I. But it almost didn't happen at all.

The Black Hand Group

The Black Hand Group was a secret society formed in Serbia in May 1911 as part of the Pan-Slavism nationalism movement, which sought to unite all Serb-populated countries, especially Bosnia and Herzegovina, which had been annexed by Austria-Hungary in October 1908.

The governor of Bosnia-Herzegovina invited Franz Ferdinand and Countess Sophie to watch his troops on maneuvers. The Black Hand Group supplied weapons to fifteen men to take part in an assassination plot during the visit. The Serbian government learned about the plan and the Serbian Minister to Vienna, Jovan Jovanovic, tried to warn the Austrian Finance Minister, Dr. Leon von Bilinski. However, his cryptic admonition that "some young Serb might put a live rather than a blank cartridge in his gun" was met with the polite response, "Let us hope nothing does happen," rather than a decisive cancellation of the trip.

New York Times.

THE WEATHER
Local showers today; Tuesday, fair; fresh, shifting winds, becoming northwest.
☞For full weather report see Page 17.

...ORK, MONDAY, JUNE 29, 1914.—EIGHTEEN PAGES.

ONE CENT In Greater New York, Jersey City and Newark. | Elsewhere TWO CENTS

ropose Pan-American
Memorial to Columbus

A splendid tomb topped by great light is proposed to ...e erected in Santo Domingo, ...n the Caribbean Sea, by sub-...riptions from peoples of all ...nds. See

...EXT SUNDAY'S TIMES.

**...R GUNS FIRE ON
SANTO DOMINGO**

...w Shots from the Machias ...top Bombardment of Puerto ...Plata by President Bordas.

...RNED BY CAPT. RUSSELL

...d Not to Endanger Foreigners in ...tack on Rebels There—Refugees Taken Off by Our Boats.

Special to The New York Times.
...ASHINGTON, June 28.—Following ...eral instructions from the Navy De-...tment to protect the lives and prop-... of Americans and foreigners in ...o Domingo, the little American gun-...t Machias on Friday afternoon ex-...d the inner harbor of Puerto Plata, ...with a few shots from her machin-...tery silenced a battery of President

HEIR TO AUSTRIA'S THRONE IS SLAIN WITH HIS WIFE BY A BOSNIAN YOUTH TO AVENGE SEIZURE OF HIS COUNTRY

Francis Ferdinand Shot During State Visit to Sarajevo

TWO ATTACKS IN A DAY

Archduke Saves His Life First Time by Knocking Aside a Bomb Hurled at Auto.

SLAIN IN SECOND ATTEMPT

Lad Dashes at Car as the Royal Couple Return from Town Hall and Kills Both of Them.

LAID TO A SERVIAN PLOT

Archduke Francis Ferdinand and his Consort the Duchess of Hohenberg

Parade Route Charade

Seven of the conspirators, men aged between seventeen and twenty-seven, lined up along the parade route on the morning of Franz Ferdinand's visit but, one-by-one, they failed to step up to the mark.

The first conspirator, a cabinet-maker named Muhamed Mehmedbašic, lost his nerve. He later claimed that he feared that a policeman standing behind him would have prevented him from throwing his bomb.

The second, a seventeen-year-old named Vaso Cubrilovic, changed his mind when the cavalcade passed because he didn't want to harm the archduke's wife. He was arrested for his part in the plot and spent sixteen years in prison, after which he became a history teacher.

The third assassin was an eighteen-year-old named Cvetko Popovic, who claimed that his eyesight failed him, so he never saw the archduke pass by.

The fourth, Nedelko Cabrinovic, plucked up the resolve to throw a bomb at the archduke's car as it passed him at 10:15 A.M., but he accidentally hit another vehicle, injuring several bystanders. He quickly swallowed a cyanide pill and jumped into a nearby canal. However, the pill was old, and he vomited it up. Because the water in the canal was only ankle deep, he was apprehended by a hysterical crowd and almost lynched.

The other three conspirators, including Princip, were unable to attack the car because of the crowds and because the car had sped up.

Hospital Visit

Franz Ferdinand decided to visit the hospital to meet some of those injured by Cabrinovic's bomb. His car was supposed to have driven along the Appel Quay to avoid the crowds, but the driver took a wrong turn, and passed Princip, who was sitting in Moritz Schiller's café eating a sandwich. As the driver was reversing slowly to correct his mistake, Princip fired several shots into the car from a range of about five feet, killing the archduke and his wife.

THE BATTLE OF THE BEES

Fought in November of 1914, the Battle of Tanga was the first major conflict in the British campaign to capture German East Africa (present-day Tanzania) during World War I. The British operation was a catalogue of blunders, mishaps, and poor leadership, culminating in British troops being attacked by swarms of angry African bees that sent them fleeing back to the beach where they had landed. This peculiar military disaster has since been nicknamed "The Battle of the Bees."

Poor Leadership

The first British mistake was the appointment of Major-General Arthur Aitken to lead the campaign. He was a colonial dinosaur who greatly underestimated his enemy and overestimated the abilities of his own troops, who were badly trained and ill-equipped. Aitken's Intelligence Officer described the troops as "the worst in India," their officers as "fossils," and remarked, "I tremble to think what might happen if we meet with serious opposition."

Before the troops set sail from Bombay to Mombassa, they were delayed for sixteen days, cooped up on a ship in overcrowded conditions and crippling heat. During the voyage, many became seasick and suffered diarrhea. Nevertheless, when they reached their destination, Aitken sent them straight on to Tanga without allowing them any time to recover.

Advance Warning

Two days before the British attack on Tanga, the British cruiser *H.M.S. Fox* sailed into the harbor and its Captain, F.W. Cauldfield, announced that the truce had been canceled. This inadvertently gave the Germans forty-eight hours to prepare for the attack: they posted snipers in trees, and set up a strong defensive position. Furthermore, Cauldfield believed the German Governor when he was told that the harbor was mined, and he persuaded Aitken to land a mile down the coast, in an inhospitable mangrove swamp. The beleaguered British troops were attacked by leeches, water snakes, mosquitoes, and tsetse flies.

As they advanced to Tanga, the British troops were picked off in large numbers by German snipers, and then ambushed. The troops fled, leaving their twelve officers to be slaughtered. By the time the British launched a second wave of troops, most were collapsing from dehydration and the German snipers continued to pick them off. Then they encountered the African bees.

The Battle of Tanga, November 3-5, 1914.

African Swarm

The African bees, large and very aggressive, had made their nest in several hollow logs that were hanging from nearby trees, and the noise of the fighting made them swarm and attack British troops. One engineer was stung over 300 times. The troops fled back to their landing beach, where a British officer remarked: "I would never have believed that grown-up men of any race could have been reduced to such shamelessness." The British soldiers were convinced that the bees were another cunning strategy of the Germans.

Naval Bombardment

The incompetent Aitken had initially refused to begin the attack with a naval bombardment (mainly because he didn't want to admit that he didn't know where the German troops were). He relented after the bee attack, but his only recorded hit was the hospital, which by now was full of wounded British soldiers. Friendly fire killed many soldiers who had escaped the enemy.

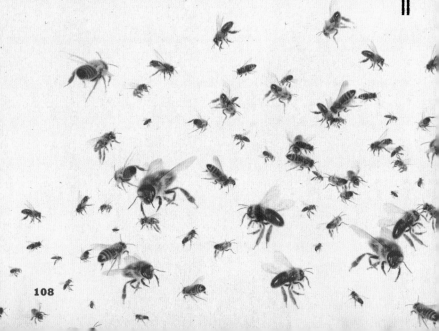

Ignoble Retreat

Finally, after casualties totaling 800 dead, 500 wounded, and 250 missing soldiers, the British sailed away, abandoning all the equipment that they had disembarked two days earlier. These supplies, including food, weapons, clothing, motorbikes, and communications equipment, enabled the German commander to equip new regiments for a year.

The Battle of the Bees was a decisive moment in the African campaign because it forced the British to reassess their enemy. The disgraced General Aitken was recalled by Lord Kitchener, the Secretary for War, who demoted him and retired him on half-pay.

THE CARVING OF THE PROTOTYPE FOR MOUNT RUSH-MORE

Each year millions of people visit the Mount Rushmore National Monument in the Black Hills of western South Dakota. It took seventeen years to carve and cost nearly $1 million dollars. The massive sculpture depicts the heads of George Washington, Thomas Jefferson, Theodore Roosevelt, and Abraham Lincoln, and is unlike any other—or is it? Two years before work began, its chief sculptor, Gutzon Borglum, had abandoned an even more ambitious project, the Stone Mountain Confederate Memorial.

Stone Mountain Confederate Memorial

The idea to carve a giant Confederate monument on the side of Stone Mountain in Georgia was conceived in 1909 by Helen Plane, the chapter president of the United Daughters of the Confederacy. She approached Gutzon Borglum in 1915, and asked him to carve a seventy-foot statue of General Robert E. Lee on the steep face of the world's largest exposed piece of granite.

He accepted the commission, but pointed out that the result would be like placing a postage stamp on the side of a barn. He proposed a more ambitious project involving a scene of Confederate greats Lee, Jefferson Davis, and Stonewall Jackson riding around the mountain with 750 soldiers. Borglum had completed a detailed model of the carving by 1917, but because of World War I the work was delayed until 1923.

Stone Mountain Confederate Memorial

Ku Klux Klan

The mountain was the site of the founding of the second Ku Klux Klan in 1915. Although part of the $250,000 for the Confederate Memorial was provided by the government, a substantial amount was raised by the Klan, and it exerted a powerful influence over the subject matter and construction. Borglum became a Klan member during his involvement with the project, which was fraught with controversy.

Disputes and Delays

Borglum faced many difficulties in realizing his vision, not least of which was how to trace the scale model onto the mountain. He solved this problem by developing a projector, and carving began on June 23, 1923, when Borglum cut the first granite himself. Within six months Lee's head was unveiled, in time for the anniversary of

his birth, but then work slowed down and Borglum fell out with the Stone Mountain Confederate Monument Association that had been formed to oversee the project. Eventually, he destroyed his model and after moving to South Carolina began work at Mount Rushmore.

Start From Scratch

Back at Stone Mountain, Augustus Lukeman replaced Borglum, but with no model to work from, Lukeman had to dynamite away Borglum's work and start over. His plans were even more ambitious than his predecessor's. He worked quickly but in three years he only managed to complete Lee's head before funds ran out and the Venable family, the previous owners, reclaimed the property in 1928. After thirty-six years, the carving resumed on July 4, 1964, and continued until March 1972. Today it is the largest bas-relief in the world.

THE GOAT-GLAND DOCTOR

In 1918, "Doctor" John R. Brinkley performed the first goat-gland transplant in Milford, Kansas, on a local farmer, to cure his sagging libido. It was the start of a quack medical empire that made him a very wealthy man and a notorious figure in the annals of twentieth-century medicine.

Early Life and Education

John R. Brinkley was born on July 8, 1885. His parents died when he was young, and he was brought up by his aunt. He attended a one-room school in Tuckaseigee, North Carolina, but he never received a diploma. Then he spent three years at the unaccredited Bennett Medical College of Chicago, but never graduated. Finally, he learned about herbal medicine at the Eclectic Medical University of Kansas City.

Pioneering goat-gland surgery wasn't his first foray into quack medicine. He had been a snake-oil salesman in a road show, and he had established

Greenville Electro Medical Doctors with a Chicago con man, James Crawford, injecting people with distilled colored water at $25 a treatment.

In 1917, Brinkley was hired as a house doctor at the Swift Meatpacking Company in Kansas. Here, he was struck by the virility of the goats that were destined for the slaughterhouse. When a farmer named Stittsworth approached him looking for a cure for impotence, Brinkley jokingly recommended some goat glands. The farmer replied, "So, Doc, put 'em in. Transplant 'em." Brinkley implanted a piece of goat gland in the farmer's testicle and after the man's wife gave birth to a baby boy (which they named

John R. Brinkley

Billy), Brinkley built a fifty-bed hospital to cope with demand for his new therapy. He charged $750 per transplant and many of his clients were delighted with results. He tried to dissuade dissenters by claiming that the operation worked the best on intelligent people and was least successful on the "stupid type."

Despite his success there were several complications. One man died of tetanus, and when Brinkley transplanted testicles from angora instead of Toggenberg goats, his patients gave off an unpleasant aroma. The medical community was quick to dismiss his work and called for his license to be revoked.

Radio Pioneer

In 1923 Brinkley set up the radio station KFKB to promote his business. He ran a program called Medical Question Box in which he offered medical advice to listeners, and was able to peddle even greater quantities of his colored water as well as other dubious herbal miracle cures. Finally, the American Medical Association persuaded the Kansas Board of Medical Registration to revoke Brinkley's license, but he merely hired licensed doctors to work in his hospital and continued to advertise with impunity from a radio station in Mexico.

To regain his license, Brinkley ran for governor of Kansas in 1930 and almost won. His empire finally collapsed after he failed to treat himself for a blood clot and had to have his leg amputated. With lawsuits piling up, he declared bankruptcy in 1941 and died the following year.

JAPANESE VOLCANO SUICIDES OF THE 1930S

On May 10, 1932, Japanese newspapers reported the suicide of Chosho Goro, a student of Keio University, and his girlfriend Yaeko. Their forbidden love culminated in an act that so captured the imaginations of other impressionable Japanese youths that over a thousand copycat suicides took place during the following year.

How Did They Die?

The young lovers met at a Christian fellowship meeting, but their relationship was forbidden by their parents because of class differences. So they climbed the Saktayama volcano above the beach at Oiso. The town is located in Kanagawa prefecture and surrounded by beautiful countryside with the south coast facing the Pacific Ocean. They left a suicide note that said they died "pure in body and spirit" and then threw themselves into the volcano's deep crater.

Media Frenzy

The copycat suicides that followed were a direct result of the romantic hysteria generated by the media. One paper in particular emphasized the Christian connection, with an article entitled "A Love That Reached Heaven." The article cleverly blended spirituality and barely suppressed eroticism, and soon the event was being re-enacted as a stage play, then a radio drama. Several sentimental songs extolling the love of Goro and Yaeko were released as sound recordings.

A Love That Reached Heaven: The Movie

Although copycat suicides were already occurring, the Shochiku Company made a movie about Goro and Yaeko whose title translates as "A Love That Reached Heaven." It was directed by Heinosuke Gosho, who had directed Japan's first talking film, *The Neighbor's Wife and Mine*, the previous year. Young couples flocked to the theaters to see the movie and many took poison while watching it. The situation got so bad that usherettes had to patrol the aisles to stop the suicides. By the end of the year several hundred youngsters had died.

Miharayama Crater

The suicides were starting to tail off when, in January 1933, nineteen-year-old student Kiyoko Matsumoto climbed Mount Miharayama, an active volcano on Oshima Island, near Tokyo, and jumped into the thousand-foot crater. Three days later the first copycat suicides began in earnest. Once again the press made a big fuss over it and even published pictures of young lovers walking up the slope, arm-in-arm, accompanied by sentimental captions. Soon tourists were gathering to watch the daily suicides, and within two years several hundred more young people had thrown themselves into the Miharayama crater.

The Werther Effect

In 1974, sociologist David Phillips gave a new name to this clustering of suicides. He called it the Werther effect, named for *The Sorrows of Young Werther*. First published in 1774, the novel tells of a young man who blows his brains out after a failed romance. The novel became a worldwide sensation, turning Johann Wolfgang von Goethe into a famous author overnight, and inspiring a spate of more than 2,000 copycat suicides.

GADSBY: A BOOK WITH NO "E"

American Ernest Vincent Wright is the author of four books. The first three were unspectacular, but the fourth, entitled *Gadsby*, was unlike any other book in the English canon. Although he described the novel as "a story of over 50,000 words," apart from the introduction and an endnote, the entire book was written without using the letter "e."

What's the Plot?

In the novel, which took 165 days to write, protagonist John Gadsby transforms his hometown of Branton Hills into a vibrant metropolis by harnessing the creative energies of its youth.

The first paragraph demonstrates his quirky and labored style:

"If youth, throughout all history, had a champion to stand up for it; to show a doubting world that a child can think; and, possibly, do it practically; you wouldn't constantly run across folks today who claim that 'a child don't know anything.' A child's brain starts functioning at birth; and has, amongst its many infant convolutions, thousands of dormant atoms, into which God has put a mystic possibility for noticing an adult's act, and figuring out its purport."

Constrained Writing

Gadsby is a lipogram (from Greek lipagrammatos, or "missing letter"), a form of constrained writing in which a letter or group of letters is omitted from a piece of writing. Every word in Wright's book is properly spelled, and every sentence makes perfect sense, but he was unable to use words like "the," "he," and "she." He also set the novel in the past tense, but was unable to use the "-ed" past tense form of any verbs.

Wright said that he had to tape down the "e" key on his typewriter so that he wouldn't make mistakes. He also resorted to convoluted descriptions of objects that he was unable to name, such as a horse-drawn fire engine. However, it seems that the mental effort required in writing such a novel hastened his death. He died in 1939 at the age of sixty-six, on the day that *Gadsby* was published, and thus never lived to see it in print.

What About Other Lipograms?

French novelist, poet, essayist, dramatist, and literary innovator Georges Perec published *La Disparition* (A Void) in 1969, without using the letter "e." He saved up all the "e"s and used them in his 1972 novel *La Disparition in Les Reventes*, in which none of the other vowels—a, i, o, and u—appear. The former was translated into English by the Scottish writer Gilbert Adair, who remained true to the original and didn't use the letter "e" either.

Ella Minnow Pea, by Mark Dunn, is described as a "progressively lipogrammatic epistolary fable." The story describes a small country that bans its subjects from using certain letters. As each letter is banned it stops appearing in the text, apart from odd occasions when characters break the law.

Georges Perec

LAST EXECUTION IN THE TOWER OF LONDON

The last person to be executed in the Tower of London was Josef Jakobs, a German spy, who was shot by an eight-man firing squad on Thursday, August 14, 1941.

Military Career

Josef Jakobs was born to German parents in Luxembourg on June 30, 1898. During World War I he served in the 4th Foot Guards as a Lieutenant. During World War II he joined the meteorological service of the German army and was secretly an officer in the Intelligence Section of the German General Staff.

Failed Spying Mission

Jakobs was captured on January 31, 1941. According to his trial statement he flew from Schipol Airport, Holland, with intentions to be dropped in the Peterborough area. Instead, he parachuted into a field at Dovehouse Farm, Ramsay

Hollow, Baldock, in Hertfordshire, after breaking his ankle on the side of the exit hole as he jumped out of the plane.

Unable to move, he fired his pistol to attract the attention of two passersby, Charles Baldock and Harry Coulson, who found him lying on his back. They immediately summoned the Home Guard, who arrested and searched him. He was carrying £500 in £1 notes and a briefcase containing a two-way wireless, headphones, and a battery. He wore civilian clothes underneath his flying suit and was carrying forged identity papers and a map with two nearby RAF stations circled in pencil.

Court-Martial

Jakobs was brought to Brixton Prison in London, where counterintelligence officers tried to recruit him as a double agent. They finally decided that he was not a suitable candidate and handed him over for a military court-martial.

Josef Jakobs was charged with "Committing treachery in that you at Ramsay in Huntingdonshire on the night of 31 January 1941/1 February 1941 descended by parachute with intent to help the enemy."

He pleaded not guilty to the charge and petitioned the King, claiming he had come to England to fight against Nazi Germany. He was found guilty and sentenced to death by firing squad.

Death at the Tower

The other German spies executed in Great Britain during World War II were hanged in civil prisons, but because a military court had tried Jakobs he was sent to the Tower of London.

On August 14, 1941, he was led to a brown Windsor chair at the rifle range (he could not stand because of his injured ankle) and a white target was pinned over his heart. At 7:12 A.M. he was shot by an eight-man firing squad composed of Scots Guards. The inquest verdict was "Execution of judicial sentence of death in accordance with military law." He was buried at St. Mary's Roman Catholic Cemetery, Kensal Green, in an unmarked grave. His death chair is still in the Tower, hidden from public view.

MAO'S SECRET FAMINE

Mao Tse-tung, the leader of the People's Republic of China from 1949 to 1976, put his people through cruel hardships to pursue his cultural and industrial reforms. Thirty million people died in the chaos caused by his inept policies. When agricultural productivity fell through the floor, peasants resorted to cannibalism, while terrified local leaders covered up the disaster to fool Mao that his utopia was a reality.

The Great Leap Forward

Mao believed that he could transform China into an industrial superpower in a few short years by ignoring expert opinion and mobilizing the entire country, fast-forwarding a process that had taken decades in other countries. Mao financed industrialization by taking central control over agriculture, so that the government could buy grain at a low price and sell it higher. The peasants were brought under control of the Communist Party by making them form into ever bigger collectives that shared tools and draft animals. At the same time that he expected major agricultural growth, Mao took tens of millions of farmers away from the land and set them to work building roads, bridges, dams, railways, and canals. The majority of these projects were rushed and poorly conceived, designed, and executed, so they were unusable. A gigantic steel industry was set up, with steel-making furnaces in every commune and in each urban neighborhood. Millions of tons of metal were confiscated from villagers, including essential farming tools, so that it could be melted down to make steel. Instead of high-grade steel, the amateur steel furnaces produced worthless pig iron.

Mao Tse-tung

Mao knew nothing about agriculture or steel production, but he insisted that food production increase, while using less land and fewer people. Provincial party leaders responded by promising to deliver impossibly high yields of grain, but when harvests fell short, they put all their energies into fooling their leader.

The Gigantic Cover-up

Grain yields were falsified by giving less to the peasants so that more could be used to meet agricultural targets. Teams of officials were sent into villages to confiscate any secret stashes of grain. The central grain stores swelled, and Mao declared agricultural production was soaring, while the peasants starved.

When Mao's higher party officials visited the provinces to view the success, local officials lined the route with newly-planted crops, and painted the bark of trees because it had been ripped off to fuel the steel furnaces, along with doors and furniture from peasant's houses. Selected peasant homes along the route were filled with grain, furniture, and other goods, to give the appearance of abundance.

Cannibalism

Meanwhile, millions of peasants resorted to cannibalism. Neighbors sold their children to each other, so that they wouldn't have to kill and eat their own offspring. Finally there were peasant revolts around the country and grain stores were raided.

H-DAY: AN ENTIRE NATION SWITCHES SIDES

Until September 3, 1967, everybody in Sweden drove on the left-hand side of the road. However, at 5:00 P.M. on that Sunday, all traffic stopped, and then everybody switched sides. "Dagen H" (H-Day) as it is known, went off without a hitch after four years of meticulous planning.

Why Did They Change?

The main argument for change was that most Swedish cars were left-hand drive. This isn't such a big problem in countries where large highways are the norm; in Sweden, however, the road network consists mainly of two-lane highways, which had caused many head-on collisions between passing left-hand drive cars. The other consideration was that Sweden's neighbors, Norway and Denmark, had always driven on the right.

Change Was Unpopular

During referenda over the previous forty years the pro-

posal to switch sides had been repeatedly voted down. For example, in a 1955 referendum only seventeen percent of people voted in favor of change. However, in 1963, the Swedish Parliament passed legislation approving the changeover and created the Statens Högertrafik-komission ("State Right-Hand Traffic Commission") to plan for its introduction. H-Day took four years of painstaking preparation, and was a logistical minefield. The State Right-Hand Traffic Commission even took the advice of psychologists.

Other preparations included introducing extra sets of traffic signals at every intersection; these were covered with black

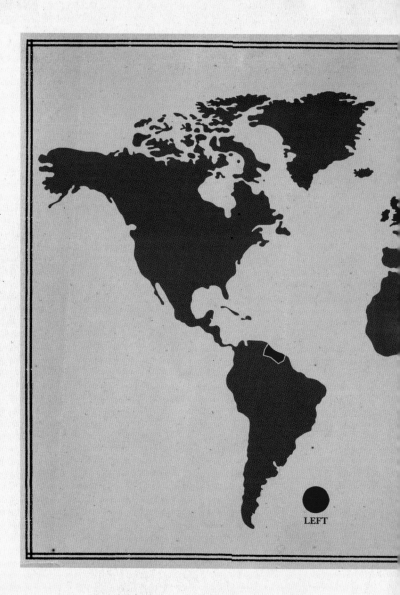

LEFT

WHICH SIDE OF THE ROAD DO YOU DRIVE ON?

RIGHT

plastic that was systematically removed on H-Day. Also, road stripes, previously yellow, were replaced by white ones, which were hidden with black tape until H-Day.

H-Day

The H stands for Högertrafik, the Swedish word for "right-hand traffic." On H-Day, only essential traffic was permitted on the roads, to reduce traffic flow to an absolute minimum. At 4:45 P.M. all vehicles had to stop and remain stationary for five minutes precisely, then change sides slowly and remain stationary again until 5:00 P.M. before driving off again. In bigger cities such as Stockholm and Malmö, non-essential traffic was banned for longer to allow intersections to be reconfigured so that traffic could merge correctly. Also, bus stops had to be erected on the opposite side of the street.

Vehicle Modifications

All vehicles had to be modified: headlights had to be adjusted so that the beam would not blind oncoming drivers; trams were discontinued and thousands of buses had to be replaced or refitted so that their doors were on the right-hand side.

Was It Any Safer?

Initially it appeared that the policy had been a success. On the Monday following H-Day, there were 125 reported traffic accidents, well below the average number of accidents for previous Mondays, and there were no reported collisions caused by the switch. Experts had predicted that driving on the right would give drivers a better view of oncoming traffic and thus reduce head-on collisions, and for a time this was the case. However, after two years the accident rate was back up to its pre-H-Day level.

THE MAN WHO WALKED AROUND THE WORLD

Dave Kunst is the first person to have walked around the entire landmass of the earth. Between June 20, 1970 and October 5, 1974, he covered 14,450 miles, in four years, three months, and sixteen days, wore out twenty-one pairs of shoes, crossed four continents and thirteen countries, and walked more than twenty million steps.

The Journey Begins

On June 20, 1970, Dave, and his brother, John Kunst, walked east out of Waseca, Minnesota, with a pack mule named Willie Makeit. They carried a plastic scroll to document the walk that would be signed by the mayor of every city and town where they spent the night. By the end of the walk there were six scrolls, covering a total area of thirty-square feet, filled with signatures.

Dave Kunst

The brothers walked to New York City and touched the Atlantic Ocean. Then they flew to Portugal and touched the Atlantic Ocean on the other side. In Europe they met Princess Grace of Monaco and presented her with one of the mule's shoes. In Yugoslavia, a villager gave them a dog which walked with them until it was killed by Turkish sheep dogs. Its replacement didn't like walking so they used a small wagon to transport it, their water, and food, and they slept in it at night. They named the wagon the "USA-Turk Machine."

Disaster in Afghanistan

Halfway around the world in Afghanistan, an Afghan newspaper reported that the brothers were collecting money for UNICEF. Soon after, in the foothills of the Hindu Kush Mountains, they were attacked by bandits who believed they would find lots of charity money in their wagon. Both men were shot and John was killed. Dave took four months to recover, and then early in 1973 another brother, Pete, joined him in the exact spot where they had been ambushed, to resume the journey.

The Khyber Pass

In Pakistan the brothers became the first non-Asians to walk through the Khyber Pass since Alexander the Great, and then they continued through India to the Indian Ocean. After touching the ocean they flew to Perth, Australia, where they were given another mule to pull their wagon. Halfway across the continent, Pete returned home and the mule died of a heart attack. Then Dave met Jenni Samuel, an Australian schoolteacher, who agreed to take the mule's place by driving alongside Dave in her car, towing the wagon. By the time they had crossed the rest of Australia together they had fallen in love, but Dave had to leave her and fly back to California for the last stage of the walk. He touched the Pacific Ocean at Newport Beach and walked across America. On the way he became the first person to walk through the underground passage at the Eisenhower Tunnel in Colorado. He reached Waseca, Minnesota on October 5, 1974, and walked into history.

Reunited

After the walk Dave returned to Western Australia to meet up with Jenni. They married the following year and returned to the U.S., where they took up residence in Orange County, California.

The Khyber Pass

INDEX